Birrias

BIRRIAS

65 Recipes from

Traditional to Modern

Jesse Valenciana

HARVARD COMMON PRESS

Quarto.com

© 2025 Quarto Publishing Group USA Inc.

Text © 2025 Jesse Valenciana

First Published in 2025 by The Harvard Common Press, an imprint of The Quarto Group,
100 Cummings Center, Suite 265-D, Beverly, MA 01915, USA.
T (978) 282-9590 F (978) 283-2742

The Harvard Common Press titles are also available at discount for retail, wholesale, promotional, and bulk purchase. For details, contact the Special Sales Manager by email at specialsales@quarto.com or by mail at The Quarto Group, Attn: Special Sales Manager, 100 Cummings Center, Suite 265-D, Beverly, MA 01915, USA.

29 28 27 26 25   1 2 3 4 5

ISBN: 978-0-7603-9269-0

Digital edition published in 2025
eISBN: 978-0-7603-9270-6

Library of Congress Cataloging-in-Publication Data available.

Cover Image: Jesse Valenciana
Design: Laura Klynstra
Photography: Clayton Hauck, , except those by Shutterstock on pages 16, 18, 21, 23, 25, 28, 32–38, 42–45,49, 50, 59, 76, 82, 83, 88–90, 94–96, 101, 105, 109, 126–128, 134, 135, 145–147, 150, 151

Printed in China

This is for my mom, whose
unwavering love, support,
and belief in me has been
my life's greatest gift.

Contents

Birrias for Every Occasion

When folks first learn about my utter obsession with birria, it comes with the assumption that my love for this traditional Mexican dish was something I had been born into. Certainly, my recipe had to be some long-held family secret; a sacred, generational gift passed down from abuelas to moms and eventually ending up in my hands under the guise of sworn secrecy. My birria fixation runs deep. The origin story of that fixation? Not so much.

I first tasted birria as a kid on a normal Sunday morning in Chicago. My dad, who threw back one too many tequilas the night before, was craving his surefire cure that would bring him right back to life: a piping hot bowl of birria and a michelada. Mexican cuisine is essentially a hangover-cure pyramid, and birria is at the top, right next to micheldas. Mexicans know that nothing cures hangovers faster than more beer.

Birria is a traditional Mexican dish that consists of a meat cooked slowly in an adobo sauce of chiles, onion, garlic, and oregano. The word *birria* can refer both to a standalone stew to be eaten on its own, with tortillas alongside for dipping, or to a sauce that is meant to be incorporated into other recipes, such as enchiladas; in this book, we use it both ways. My first bowl of birria is still vivid in my memory. I absolutely hated it. The flavor of the meat made my stomach turn, and I could have sworn I was being fed rancid beef. Unsurprisingly, my dad knew the cook that stopped by our table to say hi. He was impressed that a young kid like me had picked the goat birria. Me? Ordered goat birria? Hell no! That was my father's doing. You see, my old man wasn't exactly the progressive type that asked his kids what they wanted to eat. Nah, he took *you* with him to get what *he* wanted to eat.

I later learned that my adverse reaction to that first bowl of birria was from an underlying food trauma. Years prior, my parents had a little goat living in our basement for about a week. What I thought was going to be a family pet turned out to be the feast for a family rager in our backyard. I vowed to never eat goat again, yet here we were. Thankfully, the cook noticed me forcibly trying to please my father by eating this meat and brought me a new bowl of food. This time, it was beef birria. That first spoonful forever changed my life.

As time went on, I was consistently exposed to new cuisines from places I had read about only in schoolbooks. I have always been a curious person, so I naturally sought out food that would challenge my cooking skills while I was crafting my own recipes. My first cooking addiction was grilling, which ultimately led to my first cookbook. Street food was my next fixation that inspired a second cookbook. By this time, birria had fallen by the wayside for me. It wasn't until a chance twelve-hour, beer-fueled cooking sesh during a global pandemic reawakened my love for birria from its slumber. The birria I made that day with my social distancing partner-in-crime, Jacob Sembrano, served as a catalyst to what has become a seemingly endless food journey.

It would have been self-serving and utterly shortsighted to have set a goal of making the best birria ever. Taste is objective, so striving to make the best-tasting anything is a race to nowhere. Instead, I set off on a seemingly never-ending trek to uncover flavors, ideas, and creations with friends and peers alike. Throughout this voyage, I have repeatedly been inspired by new food I seek out and more importantly, the people around me. My hope is that with the recipes I'm sharing, these layers of flavors and creations jump out at your palate like they did mine so long ago. I want to pass on that "aha!" moment I felt when I took that fateful bite of birria that has never left my thoughts.

CHAPTER 1

The Birria Mother Recipes

BIRRIA MOTHER RECIPE NO. 1

Set it and forget it: This is the stovetop version, but if you prefer to use a slow cooker, follow the recipe through step 12, then transfer the mixture to a slow cooker, set the heat to low, and cook, undisturbed, for 12 hours.

You can also cook this recipe over live fire, but it's more of a pain in the ass to manage because charcoal is going to do its thing and keeping it at an even, low temp will be a chore. If you're up for the challenge, follow the recipe below but use a large cast-iron Dutch oven. Make sure the beef remains covered by liquid (you may need to add extra adobo, if you have it), and always keep your eye on the temperature, making sure it's between 225°F and 250°F (110°C and 120°C). It should take 3 to 4 hours.

SERVES 6

2 cups (480 ml) Beef Stock (page 50), divided

6 dried guajillo chiles

2 dried ancho chiles

1 large onion, chopped

2 cloves garlic

1 teaspoon dried oregano

1 teaspoon dried thyme

1 clove

¼ cinnamon stick

1 tablespoon (6 g) beef bouillon

2 bay leaves

4 tablespoons (60 ml) grapeseed or canola oil, divided

2 pounds (907 g) chuck roast

2 pounds (907 g) beef short ribs

Salt, to taste

Pepper, to taste

OPTIONAL TOPPINGS

Finely diced onion

Cilantro

Lime wedges

1. Bring 1 cup (240 ml) of the beef broth to a boil.

2. Meanwhile, heat a large cast-iron skillet over medium-high heat.

3. Toast the chiles for 1 to 2 minutes, turning frequently, making sure they do not burn. Discard and replace any burnt chiles.

4. Transfer toasted chiles to a heatproof bowl, add the boiling beef broth, and let the chiles soak for at least 10 minutes, or until pliable.

5. Add the onion to the cast-iron skillet and toast until the onion starts to soften and brown, about 12 minutes.

6. Meanwhile, remove the chiles from the bowl. Deseed and devein the chiles, saving the broth while discarding the seeds and veins.

7. Add the saved broth, chiles, onion, garlic, oregano, thyme, clove, cinnamon, bouillon, and bay leaves, to the base of a blender and blend until smooth. You now have adobo.

8. Heat 2 tablespoons (30 ml) of the oil in a large stockpot over high heat.

9. Strain the adobo through a fine-mesh sieve into the pot with the oil. Discard any solids left behind and cook, stirring constantly, until the adobo is the consistency of tomato paste, about 10 minutes. Set aside.

(continued)

10. Chop the chuck roast into medium-size cubes.

11. Wipe out the cast-iron pan and return it to medium heat. Add the remaining 2 tablespoons (30 ml) of oil. Add the chuck roast cubes and short ribs to the skillet and season all over with salt and pepper. Cook, stirring oven, until browned, 5 to 7 minutes. Transfer the meat to a Dutch oven.

12. Add the adobe to the meat, thoroughly covering it. Add the remaining 1 cup (240 ml) of beef stock to cover the meat.

13. Bring to a simmer and cook over medium heat for at least 4 hours, but up to 6 hours. The meat is ready when it is tender enough to start falling apart with a fork.

14. Before serving, skim the grease from the top using a skimmer spoon (see Note). Remove bones and gristle.

15. Serve your desired amount of meat in a bowl with spoonfuls of the consommé.

16. Top with finely diced onion, cilantro, and lime.

NOTE: Grease can be stored in an airtight container for up to 30 days in the refrigerator. For one way to use the leftover grease, see the Quesabirria Taco recipe on page 121.

BIRRIA DE PESCADO

This fish in birria sauce is spicy and tomatoey, but if you prefer less heat, you can decrease the number of chiles you use and/or deseed them. The fish and sauce can be served as a stew or used as a filling for tacos, topped with avocado and curtido.

SERVES 4

¼ cup (60 ml) vegetable oil, plus more as needed

10 guajillo chiles

5 Roma tomatoes

4 tablespoons (60 ml) apple cider vinegar

1 tablespoon (4 g) dried marjoram

4 bay leaves

1 tablespoon (10 g) whole black peppercorns

¼ cup (40 g) diced onion

½ whole cinnamon stick

6 large cloves garlic

6 whole cloves

1 tablespoon (8 g) ground cumin

1 tablespoon (4 g) dried ground thyme

1 tablespoon (4 g) dried Mexican oregano leaves

3 pounds (1.4 kg) whole red snapper, cleaned and deboned and cut into 4 pieces, head reserved

Salt and pepper, to taste

3 cups (375 g) all-purpose flour

Diced avocado, for garnish

Curtido (page 145), for garnish

1. Heat the vegetable oil in a Dutch oven over medium-high heat.

2. Remove the stems, devein, and deseed the guajillo chiles.

3. Add the tomatoes and guajillos to a medium stockpot, fill with enough water to cover the ingredients, and bring to a boil over high heat. Transfer the guajillos to one small bowl and the tomatoes to another. Reserve the water.

4. Add 1 cup (240 ml) of the reserved water, guajillos, vinegar, marjoram, bay leaves, black pepper, onion, whole cinnamon stick, garlic, whole cloves, cumin, and thyme to a blender and blend on high for 3 minutes or until smooth.

5. Set a fine-mesh sieve over a large bowl and pour the liquid through, using a spoon or rubber spatula to push as much of the liquid through the strainer as possible. Return the solids back to the blender along with ½ cup (120 ml) of the reserved water and blend for 1 more minute. Pour the liquid through the strainer into the large bowl again and again push as much liquid through the strainer as possible. Discard the remaining solids.

6. Blend the cooked tomatoes and the dried oregano on high for 1 minute or until smooth, then add to the liquid, stir to combine, and add salt to taste.

7. Add the tomato mixture and pepper mixture to the Dutch oven. Place the fish head in the pot along with 4 cups (960 ml) of water. Set the heat to medium and cook for 15 minutes. The mixture should not reduce or thicken.

(continued)

8. Heat a heavy-bottomed skillet over medium-high heat. Add enough oil to coat the bottom of the skillet and swirl to coat.

9. Season the fish all over with salt and pepper.

10. Add the flour to a shallow bowl. Dredge the fish in the flour, using your hands to press the flour onto the fish. Shake off any excess.

11. Arrange the fish pieces evenly throughout the pan and cook, undisturbed, on each side for 5 to 7 minutes. The fish is ready when the outside is crispy and golden brown and the inside reads 145°F (63°C) on an instant-read thermometer.

12. Transfer the fish to the Dutch oven with the sauce and cook for 15 minutes.

13. Serve in a bowl as a stew or use to make tacos topped with avocado and curtido.

CHICKEN BIRRIA

Bone-in chicken thighs are used for this recipe, as the dark meat turns juicy and succulent in the flavorful sauce. You could use boneless thighs or even breasts if you prefer; just watch carefully so they don't overcook and dry out.

SERVES 4

3 dried guajillo chiles

2 dried chiles de árbol

1 whole clove

2 tablespoons (30 ml) neutral high-heat cooking oil, such as grapeseed or canola oil

2 pounds (907 g) bone-in chicken thighs

1 teaspoon salt, plus more to taste

Pepper, to taste

1 medium white onion, quartered

2 Roma tomatoes, quartered

2 bay leaves, divided

3 cups (720 ml) chicken broth, divided

4 cloves garlic, crushed

2 teaspoons (3 g) dried Mexican oregano

1 teaspoon paprika

½ teaspoon ground cinnamon

½ teaspoon ground cumin

1. Heat a Dutch oven over medium-high heat. Add the guajillo chiles, chiles de árbol, and clove and toast for 1 to 2 minutes, turning frequently, taking care not to burn them. If any chiles do burn, discard and replace them. Transfer chiles and clove to a plate and set aside. When cool enough to handle, remove the seeds and stems from the toasted chiles.

2. Keeping the Dutch oven over medium-high heat, add the oil.

3. Season the chicken thighs all over with some salt and pepper. Add the chicken and onion to the Dutch oven. Cook for 5 to 6 minutes per side or until the onions have softened and the chicken has browned. Set aside.

4. In a large stockpot, add the toasted chiles, clove, softened onion, tomatoes, and 1 bay leaf. Cover with 2 cups (480 ml) of the chicken broth. Bring to a boil over high heat, then decrease the heat to low and simmer, uncovered, for 10 minutes

5. Remove from the heat and let cool to room temperature. Discard the bay leaf.

6. Use a slotted spoon to transfer the chiles, tomatoes, and onion to a blender, reserving the liquid for later use. To the blender, add the garlic, oregano, paprika, cinnamon, cumin, and 1 teaspoon of salt. Strain thoroughly through a fine-mesh sieve.

7. Add the reserved chicken broth and blend on high until all ingredients have blended and the mixture is smooth. Add salt and pepper to taste.

8. Return the Dutch oven with the chicken to medium heat. Add the remaining bay leaf. Pour the blended ingredients through a fine-mesh sieve over the browned chicken. Discard the solids.

9. Once the liquid begins to bubble, decrease the heat to low, cover, and simmer for 30 minutes or until the internal temperature of the chicken has reached 165°F (74°C). Remove from the heat and discard the bay leaf.

10. Transfer the cooked chicken to a cutting board and let cool for 5 minutes. Discard the skin, pull the meat from the bones, and then discard the bones. Return the chicken meat to the pot and stir to thoroughly coat.

TRADITIONAL GOAT BIRRIA

This saucy and flavorful goat birria is another favorite for using in tacos. You may need to contact a specialty butcher to get an entire goat leg; Caribbean and Spanish markets are another place to try.

SERVES 6

GOAT

3 dried ancho chiles

1 cup (240 ml) white vinegar

12 whole black peppercorns

One 1-inch (2.5 cm) piece fresh ginger

2 cloves garlic

3 whole cloves

½ teaspoon dried marjoram

1 teaspoon ground cumin

1 teaspoon dried thyme

4½ pounds (2 kg) goat leg

SAUCE

2 pounds (907 g) Roma tomatoes

2 cups (480 ml) vegetable broth

3 whole black peppercorns

2 cloves garlic

2 whole cloves

½ teaspoon dried marjoram

1 teaspoon ground cumin

1 teaspoon dried thyme

Salt, to taste

Finely chopped white onion, for garnish

MAKE THE GOAT

1. Bring a pot of water to a boil.

2. Meanwhile, deseed the ancho chiles. Once the water is boiling, add the chiles to the pot and cook for 5 minutes. Remove the pot from heat and let the chiles soak in the hot water until soft, about 10 minutes. Drain.

3. In a blender, add the softened chiles, vinegar, peppercorns, ginger, garlic, cloves, marjoram, cumin, and thyme. Blend until smooth. Place a fine-mesh strainer over a medium bowl and strain into the bowl.

4. Place the goat leg in a large bowl and pour in the chile mixture. Toss to coat. Cover and refrigerate for at least 8 hours, or up to 24.

5. When ready to cook, preheat the oven to 350ºF (180ºC).

6. Transfer the marinated meat to a baking dish; cover with aluminum foil or a lid. Bake for 3½ hours or until the meat is very tender.

7. Remove the foil and cook for another 15 minutes or until the mixture is bubbling and the meat is browned. Remove the dish from the oven, cool for 10 to 15 minutes, then pour out the meat juices into a container and reserve. Cover the baking dish with foil.

MAKE THE SAUCE

1. Meanwhile, fill a large stockpot with water and bring to a boil over high heat.

2. Add the tomatoes and boil for 7 minutes or until soft. Drain the pot and let the tomatoes cool until they can be safely handled. Peel the tomatoes and place in a blender, adding the reserved meat juices, broth, peppercorns, garlic, cloves, marjoram, cumin, and thyme. Blend on low speed for 1 minute, then increase to high and blend until smooth.

3. Transfer the broth mixture to a small saucepan, add salt, and bring to a boil over high heat. Reduce heat and simmer over low heat for 15 minutes.

4. With a fork, pull apart the meat. Sprinkle with onions and serve with a generous amount of sauce.

PORK BIRRIA

When you cook enough Mexican food, it all becomes one big Venn diagram where all creations have similarities and overlap with each other at one point or another. Pork birria is one of those. When I started making birria, I had one main adobo, and when I used it to make pork birria, I realized that it was too similar to pork chili colorado, which itself is a great dish that I highly recommend you seek out.

The main difference between birria and chili colorado is that chili colorado is a thicker stew whereas birria is thinner and has more of a consommé texture. To help differentiate my pork birria even more from a chili colorado, I changed it up from being a more traditional dried chili adobo to more of a chipotle sauce. A dry rub adds extra layers of flavor, so you will taste every ingredient in every bite of this birria.

SERVES 6

SAUCE

4 cups (960 ml) Beef Stock (page 50)

One 7-ounce (198 g) can chipotle peppers in adobo sauce

One 14.5-ounce (411 g) can fire-roasted tomatoes

1 tablespoon (10 g) minced garlic

2 bay leaves

1 teaspoon pepper

1 teaspoon ground cumin

1 teaspoon coriander seeds

½ teaspoon ground allspice

¼ teaspoon ground cinnamon

1 tablespoon (15 ml) apple cider vinegar

SPICE RUB

2 tablespoons (36 g) salt

1 tablespoon (5 g) dried oregano

1 tablespoon (7 g) onion powder

1 tablespoon (8 g) chili powder

2 tablespoons (30 ml) olive oil

MAKE THE SAUCE

1. Add all the sauce ingredients to a blender and blend until completely smooth. Set aside.

MAKE THE SPICE RUB

1. In a small bowl, mix together all the spice rub ingredients.

MAKE THE PORK

1. Rub the spice blend all over the pork. Place the meat in a slow cooker with the fat cap facing up and pour the prepared sauce over the meat.

2. Add 1 cup (160 g) of the chopped onion to the pork along with the minced garlic. Pour the vegetable broth over everything. Set the slow cooker to low and cook for at least 10 hours.

3. To serve, transfer the pork to a cutting board and use two forks to shred the meat (see Note 2).

PORK

4 pounds (1.8 kg) Boston butt or pork
   shoulder (see Note 1)

2 cups (320 g) finely chopped onion

2 tablespoons (20 g) minced garlic

2 cups (480 ml) vegetable broth

NOTE 1: For this recipe, stick to a Boston butt or pork shoulder. Do not use a picnic cut, as it will be too hammy.

NOTE 2: Save the liquid from the slow cooker. This fatty broth is perfect for making Pork Birria (page 24) or Quesabirria Tacos (page 121).

SPICY BEEF BIRRIA

Some like it hot! This is for those heat heads that want that hot spice with their birria. This recipe gives you the smoky heat from the árbol chile that bites perfectly enough and the bright green pepper heat from the serranos. Go ahead—give it a whirl!

SERVES 6

6 dried guajillo chiles

4 dried ancho chiles

6 dried chiles de árbol

2 cups (480 ml) Beef Stock (page 50), divided

1 large white onion, chopped

1 serrano pepper, roasted

2 cloves garlic

1 teaspoon dried ground oregano

1 teaspoon dried ground thyme

1 clove

¼ cinnamon stick

1 tablespoon (6 g) beef bouillon

2 bay leaves

4 tablespoons (60 ml) grapeseed oil, divided

2 pounds (907 g) chuck roast

2 pounds (907 g) beef short ribs

Salt, to taste

Pepper, to taste

Onions, for garnish

Fresh cilantro leaves, for garnish

Lime wedges, for serving

1. Heat a large cast-iron skillet over medium-high heat.

2. Add the guajillo, ancho, and árbol chiles and toast for 1 to 2 minutes, turning frequently, being careful to make sure they do not burn. Discard and replace any burnt chiles.

3. Meanwhile, in a small pot, bring 1 cup (240 ml) of the beef stock to a boil.

4. Transfer the toasted chiles to a heatproof bowl, add the hot beef broth, and let the chiles soak until pliable, about 5 minutes.

5. Return the skillet to the stove and reduce the heat to medium. Add the onion and cook, stirring often, until brown, 12 to 15 minutes.

6. Remove the chiles from the bowl. Do not discard the liquid. Deseed and devein the chiles.

7. Transfer both the reserved chile liquid and the deseeded chiles to the base of a blender. Add the serrano pepper, onion, garlic, oregano, thyme, clove, cinnamon, bouillon, and bay leaves. Blend on low until smooth.

8. Heat 2 tablespoons (30 ml) of oil in a large skillet over high heat.

9. Add the blended sauce to the oil and cook, stirring frequently, for 10 minutes or until the sauce reaches the consistency of tomato paste. Set aside.

10. Place the chuck roast on a cutting board and cut into 3-inch (7.5 cm) cubes. Season all over with salt and pepper.

(continued)

11. Next, heat a large cast-iron skillet over medium-high heat. Add the remaining 2 tablespoons (30 ml) oil.

12. Add the chuck roast and the short ribs to the skillet and cook, stirring often, until browned on all sides, about 5 minutes. Transfer the cooked beef to a Dutch oven.

13. Add the adobo and remaining beef broth to the Dutch oven and bring to a boil over high heat. Reduce heat to medium-low and simmer for 4 to 6 hours. The dish is ready when the meat is tender and easily falls apart.

14. Before serving, skim fat. Remove the meat from the liquid, discard bones and gristle and use two forks to shred the meat. Serve in a bowl with as much liquid as desired, as well as finely diced onion, cilantro and lime.

BIRRIA CONSOMMÉ

Consommé is the liquid gold that is made from the adobo, broth, and most importantly, the juices from the meat that was cooked in it. Many recipes rely on this consommé, using it as a base to layer on flavors and ingredients. But sometimes your birria may not yield enough consommé. Fear not! It's easy to stretch out the consommé you have. Just follow the recipe below.

MAKES Double the amount of consomme you already have on hand

Broth that matches the protein you are using in the birria: beef broth for beef birria, chicken broth for chicken birria, and so on

Onion, finely diced

Cilantro, chopped

1. Start by measuring how much consommé you already have. Return the consommé to the pot it was cooked in and add an equal amount of broth. Turn the heat to medium-high, add the onions, and cook until soft, about 15 minutes. Add cilantro.

BIRRIA STARTER

I used to work in the beer industry and one of the roles I held was brewery educator. It was one of the most fun jobs I ever had because I essentially got paid to learn and talk incessantly about beer. There's a process I learned about called solera aging, which is a fractional aging and blending method that originated in wine. The long and short of it, young wine is blended into older wine to allow them to mingle and age together, with the result being a magically delicious product.

Well, I took this useless info and decided to try it with the birria consommé that I was reserving from each batch of birria I was making during COVID lockdown. While everyone was trading sourdough starters, I was making birria starters. I save the birria liquid from a batch of birria and reserve it in order to use it in a subsequent batch of beef birria. What you get is a deep, rich birria every time. You can use the starter for so many other recipes: it's used in my micheladas and bloody Marias, plus the fat that rises to the top and solidifies can be used to cook your favorite dish, giving you a tasty alternative to tasteless cooking oil and/or lard.

HOW TO START YOUR GENERATION STARTER

After your beef birria is done cooking, let it cool down to room temperature. You will need to have a good amount of consommé to make a starter, so if you do not feel like you have enough, start by doubling the consommé (see page 28).

Next, make sure all of the solids have been removed from your consommé. Place a fine-mesh strainer over a large heatproof storage container or bowl. Strain the liquid. Cover. Cool to room temperature. Store in the refrigerator until cool, then move to the freezer until ready to use. You now have a first-generation starter.

As your starter sits, the fat will float to the top and form a thick, waxy seal. The fat can be used to cook with, like lard, or it can be discarded when you are ready to use your starter.

Combine your starter liquid with the adobo you use when you make a new batch of birria. I have a seventh-generation starter, and it has added a depth and richness I never knew imaginable. Keep your starter going for as many generations as you would like, making sure to keep frozen until ready to be used.

CHAPTER 2
Adobos, Salsas, and Other Sauces

CLASSIC ADOBO

This is my classic adobo sauce that you can use in many of the recipes in this book. It freezes well and is great to make in large batches.

MAKES 3½ cups (840 ml)

6 dried guajillo chiles

2 dried ancho chiles

2 cups (480 ml) Beef Stock (page 50)

1 large onion, chopped

2 cloves garlic

1 teaspoon dried ground oregano

1 teaspoon dried ground thyme

1 clove

¼ cinnamon stick

1 tablespoon (6 g) beef bouillon

2 bay leaves

2 tablespoons (30 ml) oil

Salt, to taste

Pepper, to taste

1. Heat a large cast-iron skillet over medium-high heat. Add the guajillo and ancho chiles and toast for 1 to 2 minutes, turning frequently. Discard and replace any burnt chiles.

2. Meanwhile, in a small pot, bring 1 cup (240 ml) of the beef stock to a boil.

3. Transfer the toasted chiles to a heatproof bowl, add the hot beef broth, and let the chiles soak until pliable, about 5 minutes.

4. Remove the chiles from the bowl. Do not discard the liquid. Deseed and devein the chiles.

5. Return the skillet to medium-high heat and cook the onions until they begin to brown, about 12 minutes.

6. Add the reserved liquid, deseeded chiles, onion, garlic, oregano, thyme, clove, cinnamon, bouillon, bay leaves, and remaining 1 cup (240 ml) of the beef stock to a blender. Blend on high until smooth. Strain the mixture using a fine-mesh sieve and discard the solids.

7. Heat the oil in a stockpot over medium-high heat. Add the blended sauce (adobo) to the oil, and cook, stirring frequently, until the sauce reaches the consistency of tomato paste. Season with salt and pepper to taste.

8. Allow the sauce to cool to room temperature. Transfer to an airtight container and store in the refrigerator for up to a week or the freezer for up to 2 months.

SPICY ADOBO

If the Classic Adobo (recipe opposite) is too mild for you, give this recipe a try! It will definitely bring the heat. It also freezes well, so feel free to make a large batch to store in the freezer.

MAKES 3½ cups (840 ml)

6 dried guajillo chiles

4 dried ancho chiles

6 dried chiles de árbol

2 cups (480 ml) Beef Stock (page 50)

1 large onion, roughly chopped

1 serrano pepper, deseeded and deveined

2 cloves garlic

1 teaspoon dried oregano

1 teaspoon dried thyme

1 clove

¼ cinnamon stick

1 tablespoon (6 g) beef bouillon

2 bay leaves

2 tablespoons (30 ml) oil

Salt, to taste

Pepper, to taste

1. Heat a large cast-iron skillet over medium-high heat. Add the guajillo, ancho, and árbol chiles and toast for 1 to 2 minutes, turning frequently. Discard and replace any burnt chiles.

2. Meanwhile, in a small pot, bring 1 cup (240 ml) of the beef stock to a boil.

3. Transfer the toasted chiles to a heatproof bowl, add the hot beef broth, and let the chiles soak until pliable, about 5 minutes.

4. Remove the chiles from the bowl. Do not discard the liquid. Deseed and devein the chiles.

5. Return the skillet to medium-high heat and cook the onions until they begin to brown, about 12 minutes.

6. Add the reserved liquid, deseeded chiles, serrano pepper, onion, garlic, oregano, thyme, clove, cinnamon, bouillon, bay leaves, and remaining 1 cup (240 ml) of the beef stock to the base of a blender. Blend on high until smooth. Strain the mixture and discard the solids.

7. Heat the oil in a large skillet over high heat. Add the blended chile sauce to the oil. Cook, stirring frequently, for 10 minutes, or until the sauce reaches the consistency of tomato paste. Season with salt and pepper to taste.

8. Allow the sauce to cool to room temperature. Transfer to an airtight container and store in the refrigerator for up to a week or the freezer for up to 2 months.

TOMATO ADOBO

This adobo has a more tomatoey flavor than the Classic Adobo (page 32) or Spicy Adobo (page 33). It has a milder heat and is great for freezing.

MAKES 4 cups (960 ml)

3 dried guajillo chiles

2 dried chiles de árbol

1 whole clove

3 tablespoons (30 ml) neutral high-heat cooking oil, such as grapeseed or canola oil, divided

1 medium onion, quartered

2 Roma tomatoes, quartered

2 bay leaves

3 cups (720 ml) chicken broth

4 cloves garlic, crushed

2 teaspoons dried Mexican oregano

1 teaspoon paprika

½ teaspoon ground cinnamon

½ teaspoon ground cumin

1 teaspoon salt, plus more to taste

Pepper, to taste

1. Heat a large cast-iron skillet over medium-high heat. Add the guajillo chiles, árbol chiles, and clove and toast for 1 to 2 minutes, turning frequently. Discard and replace any burnt chiles.

2. Transfer the chiles and clove to a cutting board and let cool for 5 to 10 minutes. Deseed and devein the chiles.

3. Meanwhile, heat 2 tablespoons (30 ml) of the oil in a Dutch oven over medium-high heat. Add the onion and cook until softened, about 10 minutes, then remove and set aside.

4. Add the toasted chiles and clove, softened onion, tomatoes, and bay leaves to a large stockpot set over high heat. Cover with the chicken broth. Bring to a boil, then reduce heat to low and simmer, uncovered, for 10 minutes.

5. Remove from the heat and let cool to room temperature. Discard the bay leaves. Use a slotted spoon to transfer the cooked tomatoes, onion, chiles, and clove to a blender. Add the garlic, oregano, paprika, cinnamon, cumin, and salt. Blend on high until smooth, 1 to 2 minutes. Strain. Discard the remaining solids.

6. Next, add the liquid from the stockpot to the blender and blend on high until all ingredients have blended and smoothed. Season with salt and pepper to taste.

7. Transfer to an airtight container and store in the refrigerator for up to a week or the freezer for up to 2 months.

ÁRBOL CHILE SALSA

This is an easy adobo sauce with only a few ingredients, but it does contain a lot of chiles, so beware! You can use this as a topping or leave chunky for dipping tortilla chips.

MAKES 1½ cups (390 g)

30 dried chiles de árbol

¼ cup (60 ml) white vinegar

7 whole black peppercorns

2 cloves garlic

2 white onions, minced

Salt, to taste

1. Bring a large pot of water to a boil. Add the chiles de árbol and boil until soft, about 5 minutes. Drain.

2. Add the softened chiles, vinegar, peppercorns, garlic, onions, and salt to a blender. Blend on high until smooth, 1 to 2 minutes. Strain into a bowl.

CLASSIC GUACAMOLE

This guacamole hits all the right notes: lime for acid, raw garlic for bite, and cilantro for freshness. Deseeded jalapeño brings mostly flavor with some heat. Add guacamole to as many dishes as you please. It serves as a great additional topping to tostadas, tacos, and sopes.

SERVES 6

3 ripe avocados, pitted and peeled

½ small white onion, finely diced

2 Roma tomatoes, deseeded and diced

3 tablespoons (3 g) finely chopped cilantro

1 jalapeño, deseeded and finely diced

2 cloves garlic, minced

1 lime, juiced

½ teaspoon sea salt

1. Slice the avocados in half and scoop the meat into a large mixing bowl.

2. Mash the avocado with a fork until it reaches your desired smoothness.

3. Add the remaining ingredients and stir together.

   PRO TIP: Add 1 tablespoon (15 ml) of Habanero Salsa (page 42) for a spicy kick and a whole new dimension of flavor. Want a deeper flavor? Try roasting the garlic before adding it.

ROASTED POBLANO SAUCE ("RANCHO SAUCE")

My bestie Jacob used to harass me for my disdain of ranch, so I vowed to make an all-purpose sauce that would be better than ranch. Using my favorite fresh ingredients and my preferred method of cooking (grilling), I set out to make a creation that would be as perfect for adding to a burger as it would for using as a sauce for tacos or simply for dipping potato chips in. My brain wasn't being the most clever when I decided to name it rancho, but make no mistake, this sauce will become your latest food obsession.

SERVES 14

4 poblanos

1 small white onion, quartered

1 jalapeño

4 large cloves garlic

1 cup (225 g) Kewpie mayonnaise

2 teaspoons salt

2 teaspoons cumin

1. Set the oven to broil with a rack close to the heat source. Add the poblanos, onion, jalapeño, and garlic to a sheet pan and cook for 9 minutes. Flip and cook until evenly roasted, about 3 more minutes.

2. Transfer to a heatproof airtight container with the lid securely fastened and cool for 30 minutes.

3. Under running lukewarm water, use your fingers to remove the skins, stems, and seeds from the peppers. Repeat with the skins of the onions and garlic.

4. Add the roasted poblanos, onion, jalapeño, and garlic along with the mayonnaise, salt, and cumin to a blender and blend until you have created a creamy smooth liquid.

BEACH CLUB GUACAMOLE

This recipe was born on a vacation in Tulum where I spent a long weekend on the beach subsisting on guacamole and piña coladas. I have zero regrets.

SERVES 6 to 8

3 ripe avocados, peeled, pitted, and halved

4 ounces (120 g) soft blue cheese, room temperature

⅓ cup (55 g) finely diced red onion

1 or 2 jalapeños, finely diced

3 tablespoons (3 g) finely chopped cilantro

Salt, to taste

Pepper, to taste

¼ cup (20 g) pomegranate seeds

1. In a large bowl, mash the avocados and blue cheese with a wooden spoon. A large stone molcajete would work, as well. Mash until desired consistency; chunky is this author's preferred consistency.

2. Stir in the onions, jalapeños, and cilantro. Season with salt and pepper. Sprinkle the pomegranate seeds and serve.

SALSA BORRACHA

My dad loved his hot salsa, doctors and ulcers be damned! This recipe was his go-to for when he needed his spice fix. He also swore that the secret to salsa was using a certain favorite beer of his. I say use whatever Mexican lager you have available, because until I start getting royalty checks, I'm not going to start insisting that readers use Cruz Blanca's Mexico Calling like I do.

SERVES 10

2 tomatoes

2 jalapeños

2 serranos

1 medium white onion, finely chopped

1 clove garlic

¼ cup (4 g) chopped cilantro

Salt, to taste

Pepper, to taste

2 tablespoons (30 ml) olive oil

¾ cup (180 ml) lager-style beer, at room temperature

1 tablespoon (15 ml) white vinegar

1. In a hot cast-iron skillet over high heat, cook the tomatoes, jalapeños, serranos, onions, and garlic, stirring often, until evenly charred on all sides.

2. Transfer the charred ingredients to a blender along with the cilantro, salt, and pepper. Blend on low until slightly chunky, 1 to 2 minutes.

3. Return the skillet to the heat and add the olive oil. Add the charred, blended pepper mixture along with the beer. Gently stir until combined. Cook for about 10 minutes or until the mixture has reduced and slightly thickened.

4. Add the vinegar, mix, and transfer to a glass jar to store.

This recipe calls for jalapeños and serranos, which are the two most common fresh chiles in supermarkets. They yield a medium-high heat level. But you can experiment with other chiles. Guajillo, poblano, pasilla, and ancho chiles work well, too. For a smoky accent, try chipotle, either dried or "wet" in adobo sauce.

SALSA VERDE

Salsa verde is an easy yet flavorful sauce that serves as a tool for countless Mexican dishes. If you like some heat but do not want to sweat, use a deveined, deseeded jalapeño for this recipe instead of a serrano. If you're more adventurous and want to take that heat level up a few notches, use a serrano.

SERVES 10

8 medium tomatillos, husked

4 cloves garlic, unpeeled

1 serrano or 1 jalapeño pepper

7 sprigs fresh cilantro, finely chopped

½ medium white onion, finely chopped

1 teaspoon salt

1 teaspoon sugar

1. Turn the broiler to high and place a rack about 4 inches (10 cm) from the heat source.

2. Arrange the tomatillos, unpeeled garlic, and serrano (or jalapeño) in a single layer on a sheet pan.

3. Roast, undisturbed, until browned, about 6 minutes. Turn and cook until evenly browned on both sides, about 6 more minutes. Set aside and let cool.

4. Once the ingredients are cool enough to handle, transfer the ingredients with their juices into a blender and pulse until the mixture reaches your desired smoothness.

5. Transfer the mixture to a medium bowl and stir in the cilantro and onion.

6. Season with the salt and sugar.

7. It should last up to 2 weeks if kept refrigerated.

HABANERO SALSA

This salsa will add a flavorful boost of heat to whatever you're making. From tacos to cheeseburgers, take your food to a delicious hot zone with this salsa.

SERVES 12

1 tablespoon (15 ml) olive oil

1 cup (130 g) chopped carrot

½ cup (80 g) chopped onion

5 cloves garlic, minced

6 habanero peppers, stems removed

¼ cup (60 ml) water

¼ cup (60 ml) lime juice

1 tablespoon (6 g) lime zest

¼ cup (60 ml) white vinegar

1 tomato

Salt, to taste

Pepper, to taste

1. Heat the oil in a saucepan over medium heat.

2. Stir in the carrots, onion, and garlic and cook, stirring often, until soft, about 10 minutes.

3. Transfer the mixture to a blender or food processor, add the habanero peppers, water, lime juice, lime zest, vinegar, and tomato, and blend on high until smooth, about 2 minutes.

4. Season with salt and pepper to taste. Transfer the mixture to a saucepan and simmer for 3 to 5 minutes until warm.

CERVEZA CHEESE

This beer cheese is great for topping your nachos or tacos. It is also perfect for just dipping your homemade totopos (page 151) in!

SERVES 6

2 tablespoons (28 g) unsalted butter

3 tablespoons (23 g) all-purpose flour

¾ cup (180 ml) whole milk or half-and-half

⅔ cup (160 ml) Mexican lager

1 teaspoon Worcestershire sauce

1 teaspoon Dijon mustard

½ teaspoon garlic powder

¼ teaspoon smoked paprika

¼ teaspoon salt

10 ounces (280 g) freshly grated sharp cheddar cheese (see Note)

10 ounces (280 g) freshly grated pepper Jack cheese

Cilantro, for garnish

1. Melt the butter in a medium saucepan over medium heat. Add the flour and whisk until a thick and clumpy paste forms, about 1 minute.

2. In a slow and steady stream, whisk in the milk. Continue whisking until slightly thickened, about 1 minute.

3. One at a time, whisk in the remaining ingredients.

4. Remove the cheese dip from the heat and pour into a serving dish. The dip will be thin right off the stove, but will begin to thicken after a few minutes. Garnish with cilantro.

NOTE: Make sure to shred your own cheese. Pre-shredded cheese has starch to prevent it from clumping, so it does not melt well compared with freshly shredded cheese, in my opinion.

CHIPOTLE CREMA

Mexican crema is on countless Mexican dishes. This recipe just gives that crema a kick and more of a party vibe. Out with the old, in with the new!

SERVES 12

¼ cup (60 g) Mexican mayonnaise

1 cup (230 g) sour cream

2 chipotle peppers in adobo sauce

1 teaspoon adobo sauce from can

½ lime, juiced

1 clove garlic

Pinch of salt

1. In a food processor, add the mayo, sour cream, chipotle peppers, adobo sauce, lime juice, garlic, and salt.

2. Process until the sauce becomes smooth and creamy.

HABANERO AND RED ONION CURTIDO

You can serve these the day they are made, but they are best made the day before.

SERVES 6

5 habanero peppers, thinly sliced

1 large red onion, thinly sliced

2 cloves garlic, minced

½ cup (120 ml) apple cider vinegar

½ cup (120 ml) white vinegar

½ cup (120 ml) freshly squeezed lime juice

½ cup (120 ml) water

1 tablespoon (15 g) 100% maple syrup or granulated sugar

1 teaspoon kosher salt

1. In a large bowl, combine the habaneros, red onion, and garlic. Transfer the habanero mixture to a quart jar with a lid, taking care to gently push the peppers into the jar. Leave ¼ inch (6 mm) of headspace at the top of the jar.

2. In a small saucepan, combine the remaining ingredients and heat until boiling. Remove from the burner and pour over the onions, peppers, and garlic until completely covered. Place the lid on the jar and let cool to room temperature. Store in an airtight container in the refrigerator for up to 7 days.

BIRRIA CRISP

Make when sober, but serve, if you like, with drinks.

This is a very rich and deeply flavorful condiment that is somewhere in between salsa macha and Chinese chili crisp. This recipe uses all the ingredients you would typically find in a birria recipe. This is best used as a flavor builder or enhancer on things that need a little *más sabor*. It's great on quesadillas, eggs, breakfast tacos, soups, tamales, roasted vegetables—you name it!

PRO TIP: Buy your fried garlic and onion from an Asian grocer. You have no business peeling that much garlic, slicing it, and frying it.

MAKES about 3 cups (720 ml)

CHILE FLAKES

4½ ounces (120 g) dried guajillo chiles

1¼ ounces (35 g) dried ancho chiles

AROMATIC OIL

2 cups (480 ml) avocado oil

⅓ ounce (10 g) Mexican canella

10 cloves

1 teaspoon ground coriander

1 teaspoon cumin seeds

1 teaspoon Szechuan peppercorns

1 teaspoon black pepper

10 medium bay leaves

1 teaspoon dried Mexican oregano

1 teaspoon dried thyme

1 bunch cilantro stems (cut below the leafy part)

2 bunches green onions, white part only

½ head garlic, crushed

MAKE THE CHILE FLAKES

1. Preheat a comal or heavy-bottom cast-iron skillet over medium heat. Add the dried chiles in a single layer and toast for 1 to 2 minutes per side, pressing down with a spatula for more even toasting. The peppers will soften. Toast until their color begins to change and they become aromatic. Remove from the heat and let cool just enough to handle. With kitchen shears, snip off the top, cut lengthwise, and remove the seeds and ribs; let cool.

2. With kitchen shears, cut the chiles into nickel-size pieces. Place in a blender and pulse until they become fine flakes but not powder. Discard any larger pieces that don't manage to get ground into flakes. Transfer the chili flake mixture to a small bowl and set aside.

MAKE THE AROMATIC OIL

1. In saucepot over medium-low heat, simmer all the oil ingredients for 45 minutes.

2. Strain the oil though a fine-mesh strainer or cheesecloth and return to the clean and dry saucepot. Slowly heat the oil until it reaches 325°F (170°C) on an instant-read thermometer.

(continued)

FRY AND SIZZLE

1 ounce (30 g) sesame seeds

FINISH AND SEASON

2 ounces (56 g) crispy fried garlic

¾ ounce (20 g) crispy fried onion

1 tablespoon (12 g) sugar

1 tablespoon (15 g) kosher salt

2 teaspoons MSG

1 cube beef-flavored bouillon (optional)

FRY AND SIZZLE

1. Place the chili flakes and sesame seeds in a large Pyrex or heat-resistant glass or a metal bowl. Use three-quarters of the chili flakes for a medium spice level, or use all of the flakes if you like it really spicy. Once the hot aromatic oil has reached 325°F (170°C), pour it over the ingredients. This will sizzle up multiple times the volume of the ingredients, so make sure there's enough room to accommodate for the frying.

2. Stir well and let the mixture cool down to room temperature before seasoning.

FINISH AND SEASON

1. Add the garlic, onion, sugar, salt, and MSG and mix well.

2. Crush the bouillon cube into a powder and add if you would like to, quite literally, beef up the flavor.

ESCABECHES are fairly common in Mexican cooking but they are also found in Spanish, Portuguese, French, Italian, and Filipino cooking, as well as in other parts of Latin America, in much the same form worldwide. The name *escabeche* looks and feels like a Spanish word, but its origins are in the dialect of Arabic that was spoken in Spain between the 8th and 15th centuries.

ESCABECHE

This vegetable escabeche has a garlicky, vinegary flavor that is perfect served alongside rich, fatty dishes or atop tacos, burritos, or even huevos rancheros. Cauliflower and carrots are sturdy vegetables that take well to pickling, but you could also use jicama, onions, or radishes.

MAKES about 8 cups (1.9 L)

2 tablespoons (30 ml) olive oil

1 large white onion, thinly sliced

3 large carrots, peeled and sliced

1 small head cauliflower, broken into florets

12 cloves garlic

3 large jalapeños, seeded, membranes removed, and sliced lengthwise into slivers

3 tablespoons (45 g) coarse sea salt or kosher salt

2½ cups (600 ml) water

1 cup (240 ml) distilled white vinegar

1 tablespoon (12 g) organic sugar

2 bay leaves

½ teaspoon dried oregano

½ teaspoon dried marjoram

½ teaspoon dried thyme

1. Add the olive oil to a large pot and place over medium-low heat. Add the vegetables and salt and sweat the mixture for about 10 minutes until softened. Keep the heat on the low side to avoid browning the vegetables.

2. Add the water, vinegar, sugar, and herbs and bring to a rapid boil. Cover the pot and remove from the heat to cool. When cooled, divide the mixture between two 1-quart (1 L) jars (be sure to include a bay leaf in each jar), seal, and refrigerate for a minimum of 3 days before serving. (Refrigerated escabeche will last for a few months stored in this manner.)

3. To seal the jars and preserve the escabeche for pantry storage, remove the pot from the heat. Carefully divide the hot mixture between two 1-quart (1 L) mason jars (be sure to include a bay leaf in each jar). Put the lids in place and tighten the lid rings. Invert the jars for 10 minutes. After 10 minutes, turn the jars upright and slightly loosen the lid rings. Let the jars rest and cool until the lids "pop" and seal shut. Retighten the lid rings and store the jars in the pantry until ready to use.

BEEF STOCK

Homemade beef stock is time-consuming, but it's a most rewarding endeavor as when you're entering the world of birria, you'll find out just how important good beef stock is for your creations.

MAKES 5 to 6 cups (1.2 to 1.4 L)

4 to 5 pounds (1.8 to 2.3 kg) beef scraps such as marrow, bones, or oxtail

1 pound (455 g) beef stew meat (or additional 1 pound [455 g] beef scraps), cut into 1-inch (2.5 cm) chunks

1 medium onion, quartered

Vegetable oil

5 cloves garlic, unpeeled

Fresh cilantro, including stems and leaves

3 tablespoons (16 g) dried Mexican oregano

3 bay leaves

10 peppercorns

BLANCH THE BONES

1. Add the beef scraps to a large stockpot and cover with cold water. Bring to a boil over high heat, then reduce heat to medium and simmer aggressively for 20 minutes. Remove the pot from the heat and drain the water.

ROAST THE MEAT

1. Preheat the oven to 450°F (230°C).

2. Pat the beef dry. Transfer the meat, garlic, and onions to a large, shallow roasting pan and drizzle with the oil. Toss to coat.

3. Roast for 20 minutes. Remove the pan from the oven, flip the meat, and return the pan to the oven. Cook for 30 minutes or until ingredients are brown but not burnt. If bones begin to char at all during this cooking process, lower the heat to 350°F (180°C).

4. Remove pan from the oven and transfer the ingredients to a 12-quart (11 L) or larger stockpot.

5. Meanwhile, bring 2 cups (480 ml) of water to a boil in a small pot. Pour the water over the pan and use a wooden spoon to scrape up any browned bits. Transfer the liquid and brown bits to the stockpot with the beef and onions.

SIMMER THE STOCK

1. Add the cilantro, oregano, peppercorns, and bay leaves to the stockpot. Fill the stockpot with cold water until the bones are covered by 2 inches (5 cm) of water. Bring to a boil over high heat, then reduce to low and simmer, loosely covered, for at least 6 hours and up to 12 (I prefer the longer time).

2. As the stock is cooking, fat will be released from the bones and meat. Use a slotted spoon to remove and discard the fat that rises to the top as you occasionally check in on the stock.

STRAIN THE STOCK

1. When cooking is complete, with a slotted spoon, carefully and gently remove and discard bones, meat, and vegetables.

2. Line a strainer with cheesecloth. Add 2 to 3 cups (300 to 450 g) of ice to a shallow pan, then pour the stock through the cheesecloth-lined strainer. Discard the solids.

COOL THE STOCK

1. Carefully cooling down the stock is of utmost importance as hot broth can be a breeding ground for bad bacteria. Using a shallow pan for the stock will aid it in cooling down faster. Keep the stock in the shallow pan. Cool until room temperature. Cover and transfer to the refrigerator for 3 hours.

2. Remove the pan from the refrigerator. Any remaining fat should be solidified on the surface. Carefully scrape it off and discard.

3. At this point, you should have a wonderfully jiggly stock that will be ready for use. Add to a storage container and refrigerate. If you don't plan on using it right away, you can freeze it for up to 3 months.

Breakfast Birrias

BIRRIA-QUILES

Mexico City is one of my favorite places in the world. It is such a culturally rich city, and the food is on a whole other level. One of my absolute favorite things to eat in Mexico City is chilaquiles. The city has no shortage of places that on any given day can whip up a mind-blowing version of this brunch dish. This recipe is no substitute for a trip down there, but I'd say it's a close second.

MAKES 4 chilaquiles

Vegetable oil

12 cold or stale 6-inch (15 cm) corn tortillas, cut into wedges

4 cups (960 ml) Birria Consommé (page 28)

2 cups (480 g) Birria Mother Recipe No. 1 (page 15), drained

½ cup (115 g) Mexican crema

½ large white onion, thinly sliced

¼ cup (30 g) grated queso añejo

4 sunny-side up eggs

FRY THE TORTILLAS

1. Heat 1 inch (2.5 cm) of vegetable oil in a large skillet over medium-high heat.

2. When the oil is hot enough to make a tortilla wedge sizzle, it is ready. If you have a thermometer, it should read 350°F (180°C).

3. Add tortilla wedges and fry for 3 minutes; when the wedges have stopped bubbling, they should be ready.

4. Remove the chips with a slotted spoon or tongs and transfer to a sheet pan lined with paper towels.

5. Discard all but ¼ cup (60 ml) of oil from the frying pan.

PREPARE THE SAUCE

1. Keep the oil-filled skillet on the heat and add the consommé. Bring to a full boil.

2. Add the tortilla chips and birria. Gently stir until coated with sauce.

3. Turn off the heat, cover, and let stand for 3 to 5 minutes until the tortillas have softened to your liking.

4. Gently stir everything together, then scoop into deep plates for serving.

5. Drizzle with the crema, scatter on the onion slices, and sprinkle generously with cheese.

6. Add a sunny-side up egg to the top of each plate and serve.

BIRRIA BREAKFAST BURRITOS

If you're ever in Nashville, make it a point to find these breakfast burritos. I have a business called the Secret Bodega, and we make literally hundreds of these each week for accounts all over the city. If you don't want to buy a plane ticket or have to fight the crowds of drunken bachelorettes in Nashville, you can just make this recipe at home.

MAKES 2 burritos

Two 10-inch (25 cm) Flour Tortillas (page 135)

⅔ cup (160 g) Spicy Beef Birria (page 27)

3 large eggs

1 tablespoon (15 ml) heavy cream

1 tablespoon (14 g) butter

6 tablespoons (45 g) Chihuahua cheese

Salt, to taste

Pepper, to taste

2 tablespoons (30 g) Pressure Cooker Refried Beans (page 146)

12 frozen potato puffs, air-fried

Chipotle Crema (page 44)

PREPARE THE TORTILLAS

1. Heat a medium nonstick skillet over high heat. Add the tortillas one at a time and cook until slightly crispy and brown, about 30 seconds per side. Transfer the warmed tortillas to a plate and cover with a tea towel. Set aside.

2. Reduce the heat to medium and add the birria. Do not shake off the consommé. Cook, stirring frequently, until warmed through and steamy. Turn off the heat and let the meat rest.

COOK THE EGGS

1. In a medium bowl, mix together the eggs and heavy cream.

2. Pour the egg mixture into a nonstick skillet, add the butter, and turn the heat to medium.

3. Using a spatula, stir the eggs constantly as the butter slowly melts, scraping the bottom of the pan all over in a long, continuous motion. Do this for about 10 minutes until eggs are set.

4. Add the cheese, stir, and remove from the heat. Eggs should be custardy-looking, but not runny.

5. Season to taste with salt and pepper.

(continued)

ASSEMBLE THE BURRITOS

1. Portion out the birria and potato mixture into 2 servings.

2. Divide the birria filling evenly for the 2 burritos. Start by spreading the beans down the middle of the tortilla, and follow by adding 6 potato pieces over the beans and layering the remaining ingredients on top of each, making sure to add the cheese last.

3. Heat the large skillet over medium heat.

4. Fold and roll the burritos, then place them in the pan seam side down and cook until the tortilla has browned, about 3 minutes per side.

5. Serve with chipotle crema.

If you or your guests are not fans of beans for breakfast, you can omit them from the recipe and replace them with 2 extra tablespoons of Spicy Beef Birria (31 g) or Chihuahua cheese (15 g). If you do decide to leave the beans out of the burritos, you still can serve them alongside the burritos. If you do, double the amount to 4 tablespoons (60 g) of beans.

"MEXICAN TIME" SCRAMBLED EGGS

I would spend my summers in Mexico, in the city of Torreón in the state of Coahuila, when I was a kid. Breakfast was always forgettable scrambled eggs, some random protein, and corn tortillas. The tortillas were the absolute star of the show. I can still smell the aroma that used to waft into the kitchen every morning from the tortilleria that was in the house right next door. The tortillas were essentially utensils more so than a vessel for the food on the plate, but they were the best part.

When I finally learned to make my own tortillas, I was armed with what I feel is the best birria, so the next step was to learn how to make the best scrambled eggs. Enjoy these eggs with some beef birria and freshly made corn tortillas. Add a splash of habanero salsa and you're essentially reliving my summers in Torreón.

SERVES 2

3 large eggs

1 tablespoon (15 ml) heavy cream

1 tablespoon (14 g) butter

Salt, to taste

Pepper, to taste

1. In a medium bowl, mix together the eggs and heavy cream. Do not overmix.

2. Pour the egg mixture into a nonstick skillet, add the butter, and turn the heat to medium.

3. Using a spatula, stir the eggs constantly as the butter slowly melts, scraping the bottom of the pan all over in a long, continuous motion. Do this for about 10 minutes until eggs are set.

4. Remove from the heat. Eggs should be custardy-looking, but not runny.

5. Season with salt and pepper.

BIRRIA BREKKIE TACOS

These brekkie tacos are a hearty breakfast meant for enjoying. Be ready for a post-breakfast siesta after eating these.

MAKES 4 tacos

2 medium red potatoes, diced

3 tablespoons (45 ml) Birria Consommé (page 28)

1 cup (240 g) Birria Mother Recipe No. 1 (page 15)

4 Flour Tortillas (page 135)

4 large eggs

2½ tablespoons (38 ml) olive oil

Árbol Chile Salsa (page 35)

Crumbled queso fresco

3 tablespoons (3 g) cilantro leaves

½ medium white onion, finely diced

COOK THE POTATOES

1. Fill a large saucepan about two-thirds full with water, heavily salt, and bring to a boil over medium-high heat.

2. Add the potatoes and cook for 8 minutes or until completely tender but not falling apart.

3. Heat a large cast-iron skillet over medium-high heat. Add the consommé along with the birria. Cook, stirring frequently, until the consommé begins to steam and thicken, about 10 minutes.

4. Stir in the potatoes, reduce the heat to low, and cook, stirring often, until tender, about 10 minutes.

5. Remove from the heat.

WARM THE TORTILLAS

1. Bring a clean, large nonstick pan up to high heat and warm up the tortillas. Cook until crisp and brown, about 30 seconds per side. Transfer the warmed tortillas to a plate and cover with a tea towel. Set aside.

COOK THE EGGS

1. Heat the olive oil in a large nonstick pan over medium-low heat. When the oil shimmers, add an egg, cook for 45 seconds, then flip and cook for 25 more seconds. Remove from the heat and set aside. Repeat with the remaining eggs.

ASSEMBLE THE TACOS

1. Divide the birria mixture evenly among the tortillas. Place 1 egg on top of each tortilla. Spoon desired amount of árbol chile salsa on each tortilla and sprinkle each with queso fresco, cilantro, and onions.

MOLLETES

Growing up, my mom used to whip together a breakfast dish that was essentially a birria and bean sandwich. I used to think she was some kind of breakfast wizard, making magic out of leftovers. When I visited Mexico City as an adult, I realized that my mom was simply making molletes, which are a breakfast staple in Mexico.

They were so simple yet so delicious, and me being me, I couldn't leave this recipe alone. I played around with various cheeses to use on my molletes until I settled on aged Manchego. The nuttiness of this cheese really plays well with the rest of the ingredients. I also used chicken birria for this creation because based on my experience in Mexico City, I felt beef was a bit too heavy for a breakfast dish.

MAKES 6 molletes

1½ cups (360 g) Chicken Birria (page 20), warmed

3 bolillos or thick, crusty sandwich rolls

1 cup (240 g) Pressure Cooker Refried Beans (page 146)

6 slices aged Manchego cheese

Mexipoix (page 147)

Sliced avocado, for serving

1. Turn the oven on to broil.

2. Cut the bolillos or rolls in half and butter the inside of both sides. Broil buttered side up for 2 minutes or until lightly toasted.

3. Evenly spread the beans onto the buttered side of the bolillos and add a slice of Manchego cheese to each one.

4. Place back under the broiler for 5 minutes or until the cheese is melted evenly.

5. Remove from the broiler and divide the birria between the sandwiches, spooning it over the melted cheese. Top with Mexipoix and sliced avocado.

CHAPTER 4

Dishes with a Birria Base 1: Mexican and Mexican-Inspired

BIRRIA FLAUTAS

Flautas were a staple in my household growing up. Traditionally, flautas are dressed and served on a plate. Recently, my partner Audrey had the idea to serve them in a cup, which transformed the dish from a sit-down affair to a snack you can walk around with and eat at your leisure, like you are at a country fair watching unsupervised kids scream their heads off on a questionably safe ride while drinking an increasingly warm beer in the sweltering summer heat. It has become our favorite way to enjoy flautas.

MAKES 10 flautas

4 cups (960 g) Chicken Birria (page 20)

1½ cups (175 g) shredded Chihuahua or Monterey Jack cheese

½ cup (120 ml) Salsa Verde (page 41)

1 cup (160 g) finely chopped onion

10 corn tortillas

1 quart (960 ml) vegetable oil for frying

½ cup (115 g) sour cream (optional)

½ cup (120 g) Classic Guacamole (page 36) (optional)

Vinegar-based hot sauce (optional)

Lime slices, for garnish (optional)

1. In a medium bowl, mix together the shredded chicken, cheese, salsa verde, and onion.

2. Add about 1½ tablespoons (23 g) of the chicken, cheese, and onion mixture to each tortilla. Do not overfill. Roll tortillas and secure with toothpicks.

3. Line a plate with paper towels.

4. In a Dutch oven or deep, heavy frying pan, heat oil to 350°F (180°C).

5. Add the rolled tortillas to the skillet in a single layer, being careful to leave space between each. You may need to work in batches. Cook until golden brown and crisp, 3 to 5 minutes total. They should float for about a minute before they are ready.

6. Transfer the finished tortillas to the prepared plate until ready to serve.

7. Serve the flautas straight up or with the sour cream, guacamole, and hot sauce alongside. For an upscale presentation, fill 3 to 5 glasses with sour cream and guacamole. Drizzle the flautas with hot sauce, then distribute them vertically among the glasses. Garnish, if you like, with lime slices and additional shredded cheese.

BIRRIA PUFFS

Maíz de la Vida is an authentic, craft tortilleria in Nashville, Tennessee. I swung by one day to pick up some fresh flour tortillas (don't worry, corn tortillas are their main product being produced). I had an event coming up and I had a pizza puff on my menu. Pizza puffs are a Chicago fast-food staple that doesn't get the hype that Italian beefs and Chicago dogs do but are worthy of its space in the pantheon of Chicago fast-food treasures. Pizza puffs are flour tortillas filled with pizza ingredients. The guys couldn't wrap their heads around this concept, as I swore to them the deliciousness of it. I figured I would make a puff of sorts on the spot, so I grabbed some cheese and some of their delicious birria and made do. What was born that day is hands-down one of the tastiest happy accidents a kitchen has ever had. Now you can make it at home.

MAKES 4 puffs

4 Flour Tortillas (page 135)

2½ cups (280 g) shredded Chihuahua or Monterey Jack cheese

2 heaping cups (480 g) shredded Birria Mother Recipe No. 1 (page 15), with most of its juice squeezed out

1 tablespoon (8 g) all-purpose flour

1 tablespoon (15 ml) water

1 cup (140 g) Mexipoix (page 147)

Hot sauce, for serving

1. In a Dutch oven set over medium-high heat, bring about 3 inches (7.5 cm) of oil to 375°F (190°C).

2. Place the tortillas on a flat surface, place ¼ cup (30 g) of the Chihuahua cheese in the center of the tortilla, top with a heaping half cup of birria, and add a large pinch of Chihuahua.

3. In a small bowl, mix together the flour and water. Fold the tortilla into a tight, neat square and secure the ends by brushing with the flour-water mixture.

4. Add the filled tortillas to the oil and cook undisturbed for 3 to 4 minutes. Flip and cook until golden brown, 3 to 4 more minutes. The puff will float when done.

5. Allow to cool slightly, top with the Mexipoix, and serve with hot sauce on the side.

BIRRIA SMASHBURGERS

If memory serves me right, my obsession with birria coincided with the smashburger boom that swept the nation, which also coincided with my move down to Nashville, Tennessee. Smashburgers seemed to be everywhere, but there was one pop-up that seemed to reign supreme: Bad Luck Burger Club. They were like some rad, secret burger society that everyone was privy to. The burgers they were slinging were addictive little bundles of deliciousness, and I was immediately inspired by their vibe, energy, and most importantly, their burgers.

Not long after moving to town, I was invited to do a pop-up at a local brewery, so the stage was set for me to finally share my smashburger creation with other folks. The birria smashburgers were an instant hit, and I sold out almost immediately. Every time I have added this recipe to the menu at one of our pop-ups, it's been the crowd favorite, and when I'm cooking burgers for pals, this will always be in the rotation.

MAKES 2 burgers

12 ounces (340 g) 80/20 ground beef

Salt, to taste

Pepper, to taste

⅔ cup (160 g) Birria Mother Recipe No. 1 (page 15)

⅔ cup (76 g) shredded Mexican cheese blend

2 hamburger buns

1 cup (55 g) finely shredded lettuce

2 slices tomato

½ cup (70 g) Mexipoix (page 147)

4 tablespoons (60 ml) Roasted Poblano Sauce (page 37)

1. Preheat a griddle to 450°F (230°C).

2. Divide beef into 4 equal portions. Roll each portion in the palms of your hands to form a ball.

3. Place the balls on the griddle in a single layer with ample space between them.

4. Place a piece of parchment paper over the first ball, and use your burger press or a stiff spatula to press down until the burger patty is evenly thin and flat. Once the burger is smashed, apply pressure using the press or spatula for about 10 seconds. Repeat the process until all 4 burgers are smashed. Remove the parchment paper.

5. Season the top side of each patty with salt and pepper to your liking. No need for any store-bought burger seasoning.

6. Dab the inside part of the hamburger buns in the residual grease on the griddle, and toast the buns while the burgers continue to cook. When the buns are done toasting, remove them from the griddle.

(continued)

7. When the patties are a bit more than halfway cooked through (and there are still some pink spots on top), use a very thin spatula or scraper to scrape under the cooked burger crust and flip the patty to the uncooked side.

8. Immediately after flipping the burger patties, prepare the cheese blanket by placing ⅓-cup (40 g) rounds of shredded cheese on the hot griddle.

9. Stack 2 burger patties on top of each other to make 2 double smashburgers and top with birria.

10. When the cheese begins to caramelize, forming a thin crust, and the top side is melty, scrape off to place on top of the burger stacks.

11. Remove the smashburgers from the griddle and transfer to the prepared buns. Serve warm.

12. Each bottom bun should get a layer of shredded lettuce, a tomato slice, 2 burger patties, Mexipoix, and a healthy amount of Roasted Poblano Sauce.

BIRRIA SMOKED SAUSAGES

My buddy Bob Delay is the sausage king of Nashville, with 10 years of experience making sausage. Bob moved to Nashville several years ago and found out there was a street-food obsession with all things birria, especially tacos. When I informed Bob that I was writing a new cookbook focused on birria, he jumped at the opportunity to create a birria smoked sausage and we're all lucky for that. You can easily substitute beef instead of lamb, but Bob particularly enjoys using the more traditional lamb meat in a sausage since it holds its flavor better with the mesquite smoke.

MAKES 20 (4-ounce) sausage links

SAUSAGE

5 pounds (2.3 kg) lamb (see Note 1)

2 tablespoons (30 g) kosher salt

1 teaspoon (5 g) cure #1 (also known as Insta Cure #1, Prague powder #1, or pink cure #1)

1 tablespoon (10 g) ancho chile powder

1 teaspoon guajillo chili powder

1 teaspoon chile de árbol powder

1 tablespoon (10 g) onion powder

1½ tablespoons (15 g) garlic powder

1 teaspoon ground cinnamon

1 teaspoon black coarse pepper

1 teaspoon allspice

1 teaspoon dried (Mexican) oregano

½ teaspoon ground cumin

1½ teaspoons paprika

1½ ounces (40 g) dry powdered milk (soy powder can be used as an alternative)

½ cup (120 ml) ice water

24 to 26 mm hog casings

TO SERVE

Sausage rolls

Diced onion

Chopped cilantro

MAKE THE SAUSAGE

1. Grind lamb through a $3/16$-inch (5 mm) plate (see Note 2).

2. In a large mixing bowl, stir together the ground lamb, seasonings, milk powder, and water. You should have a sticky mixture. Cover and refrigerate overnight.

3. Stuff firmly into the hog casings and form 6-inch (15 cm) links.

4. Hang sausages to dry until the casing is sticky to the touch. Drying the sausages brings them to about the same temperature for an even smoke color. It also conditions the surface of the sausages to ready them to accept smoke and causes a "skin" to form on the outside surface of the sausage. Drying also gives the casing strength to hold up during cooking.

5. Smoke sausages at 200°F (100°C) until the internal temperature reaches 160°F (71°C [see Note 3]).

SERVE

1. Serve on your favorite artisanal sausage roll and top with diced onion and chopped cilantro.

NOTE 1: We're going for a 70/30 ratio of meat to fat, so shank or leg works best.

NOTE 2: Before grinding, partially freeze the lamb.

NOTE 3: I suggest mesquite wood for this recipe.

BIRRIA TAMALES

My friend Marisa Celise Torres, aka Tamale Lady, once took some of my birria to mess around with as most food creatives do. She made a few tamales for me and apologized because she had run out of Oaxacan cheese, so she substituted it for some queso she had made for an upcoming event of hers. For those that don't know, Nashville folks treat queso like liquid gold, and before I had these tamales, I never really cared for it. These tamales were ridiculous and easily the cheesiest tamales I have ever tasted. You can make these with Oaxacan or Chihuahua cheese. Not me though—I'm never going back. It's queso or nothing for me. (Sorry, grandma.)

MAKES 12 tamales

CORN HUSKS

One 6-ounce (170 g) package corn husks

DOUGH

6 cups (756 g) blue or white masa

1 tablespoon (12 g) baking powder

¾ cup (180 ml) avocado oil

6 cups (1.4 L) vegetable stock

TAMALES

4 cups (960 g) Pork Birria (page 24)

3 cups (120 ml) Nashville Queso (page 150)

SOAK THE CORN HUSKS

1. Soak the corn husks in hot water for 30 minutes.

MIX THE DOUGH

1. In a large bowl, add the masa and baking powder and whisk to combine.

2. Add the oil, mix until evenly combined, then gradually add the stock ½ cup (120 ml) at a time.

ASSEMBLE AND COOK THE TAMALES

1. Lay a corn husk, glossy side up, on a table with the wide end at the top. Scoop about ¼ cup (60 g) of dough onto the center of the top half of the corn husk.

2. Lay a piece of plastic wrap over the dough and use your hands to press and spread the masa into a thin layer, about ¼ inch (6 mm) thick.

3. Keep the dough spread along the top half of the corn husk to allow plenty of room to fold the bottom husk up.

4. Add ⅓ cup (80 g) of birria and ¼ cup (120 ml) of queso to the center of each tamale

5. Fold in one long side of the husk over the filling. Fold in the other long side, overlapping the first (like folding a brochure). Fold the bottom of the husk up.

(continued)

6. Add water to the bottom of an electric pressure cooker. Lay a few extra corn husks on the bottom rack to keep the tamales from falling through and any boiling water from directly touching them.

7. Place tamales standing upright, with their open end up, just tightly enough to keep them standing. Cook on high pressure for 25 minutes. Allow pressure to naturally release for 10 minutes, and then quick release. To test if the tamales are done: Remove one and try to pull the husk off. If the husk pulls away cleanly from the tamale, they're done. If the dough is still sticky or wet-looking, cook for 5 to 10 minutes longer.

AUDREY'S EMPANADAS

My partner Audrey is a hell of a cook. When we first started dating, I thought I would be able to impress her with my creations only to be shown up by her kitchen prowess. After that, I sat back and let her take the wheel when it would come to cooking. I obviously have days where I get to cook for her, but for the most part, she's the kitchen boss!

We were invited to do a pop-up, and Audrey had the great idea to make empanadas, which was brilliant because they were pretty and delicious and definitely a winning combo. We have made our own empanada dough, but trust us, there are empanada dough discs that are just as great and will save you time and energy. That's our collective pro tip.

MAKES 10 empanadas

1 large egg

1 teaspoon water

Flour

10 frozen empanada dough disks

1¼ cups (300 g) Birria Mother Recipe No. 1 (page 15)

1¼ cups (150 g) shredded Chihuahua cheese

Birria Consommé (page 28) or Salsa Verde (page 41), for serving

1. Thaw the frozen empanada dough by following the instructions on the packaging.

2. Preheat the oven to 400°F (200°C).

3. Whisk together the egg and water to create an egg wash. Set aside.

4. Drape a damp paper towel over the empanada dough (see Note 1).

5. Set a dough disk on a flat, lightly floured surface. Add 2 tablespoons (30 g) of birria and 1 to 2 tablespoons (8 to 16 g) of shredded Chihuahua cheese to the center of the empanada disk (see Note 2).

6. Using your finger or a pastry brush, lightly coat the exposed edges of dough with the egg wash and fold in half to seal. The egg wash will act as a glue to keep the dough from splitting open.

7. Pinch and twist the edges of the dough to create a rope-like texture for a classic empanada finish. You can also press the back of a fork into the edges to seal.

8. Repeat with the remaining ingredients.

9. Lightly brush the whole surface of each empanada with the remaining egg wash. This will create a golden sheen while baking.

(continued)

10. Place the empanadas on a parchment paper–lined baking sheet. Bake for 20 minutes or until golden brown (see Note 3).

11. Serve while warm with consommé or salsa verde.

NOTE 1: The dough will quickly dry out and become difficult to work with if left uncovered.

NOTE 2: It's easier to seal an empanada that isn't overstuffed, so the amount of filling you use will vary depending on the size of the disk.

NOTE 3: To cook with an air fryer, preheat to 400°F (200°C). Generously spray the surface of the air fryer basket with nonstick spray. Add empanadas in a single layer and cook for 10 minutes or until golden brown, flipping halfway through. You may need to work in batches.

The Spanish word for bread is *pan*, and *empanada* simply means, in both Spain and Latin America, any food that is breaded or encased in bread, much like the French *en croute*. The most common use of empanadas, however, is specifically for these small and usually meat-filled pasties.

BIRRIA ROULADE TORTAS

Here is a recipe from my friend John Scholl, who contributed this introduction: "You've conquered the art of birria with a recipe straight out of this fantastic book, but now you find yourself swimming in a sea of savory leftovers. Fear not, for I am the reigning champion of utilizing excess provisions by creating more excess! We could stick to the conventional indoor cooking routine, but where's the thrill in that? Let's take our culinary escapades outdoors, where the flames dance, and the aroma of smoky goodness fills the air that will make your neighbors jealous. It's time to unleash your primal instincts and roll up some meat with meat over a live fire!"

MAKES 8 tortas

2-pound (910 g) pork loin

1½ cups (360 ml) Birria Consommé (page 28), divided

2 cups (480 g) Birria Mother Recipe No. 1 (page 15), shredded

1 cup (120 g) shredded Chihuahua cheese

Butcher string, for trussing

8 telera rolls or bolillo buns

2 cups (70 g) shredded lettuce

2 tomatoes, sliced

Hot sauce, to taste

Mexican mayonnaise, to taste

1. Prepare the pork loin by butterflying. You'll want to slice thinner than the traditional cut down the middle to butterfly so the loin rolls better. The goal is to get it as thin and wide as possible so you can stuff it with delicious birria and cheese. I typically start about a third down from the top and cut 90 percent of the way through length-wise. Think of it like you're opening a book. Next, rotate the loin and cut another third, essentially opening another side like a book. What you end up with should be a nice wide and even piece of pork.

2. Place the pork in a bag or nonprous container. Immerse the pork in 1 cup (240 ml) of the consommé and marinate for 12 hours, flip, and marinate for 12 more hours.

3. Set up the grill for indirect cooking at 400°F (200°C).

4. Remove the pork from the marinade and lay flat on a cutting board. Spread the birria across the butterflied loin and then top with cheese. Roll this baby up. It will be much fatter than the original loin because you're stuffing it, so use the butcher string to truss the meat so it stays together while grilling.

(continued)

5. Place the meat on the grill and give it a quarter turn every 3 to 4 minutes until the internal temperature reaches 165°F (74°C). This will take around an hour, so grab a beer and a chair to enjoy the weather. Brush the meat with the remaining ½ cup (120 ml) of consommé throughout the grilling.

6. Once the meat reaches temperature, place it on a wire rack and let it cool for 10 minutes.

7. Slice or chop the meat; it's your house, so cut the meat however you want. Place the meat on the buns and top with lettuce, tomatoes, hot sauce, and mayo.

WANNABE CELEBRITY BIRRIA DOGS

There used to be an iconic restaurant in Chicago that was dubbed an "encased meat emporium," by its beloved owner/operator, Doug Sohn. Doug is a friend, and I've never told him, but I have always looked at him like a mentor. So much so that I have a tattoo on my right butt cheek of the logo of his now closed sausage superstore, Hot Doug's.

Doug made art with his encased meat creations. One of my favorite food claims to fame was having helped create a Sonoran hot dog, along with my great friends, John Scholl and John Caruthers, that made it on the Hot Doug's "Celebrity Dog" menu. This was one of the highest wiener honors ever bestowed upon a mere mortal. I so wish Hot Doug's was still open for a multitude of reasons: most importantly because I would love to be welcomed by Doug with his usual, "What can I get you, my friend?" but also because I think this creation would have totally killed it as a Celebrity Dog.

MAKES 5 hot dogs

2 tablespoons (30 ml) grapeseed or canola oil

6 beef hot dogs

2 cups (240 g) shredded Mexican cheese blend

6 hot dog buns

2 cups (480 g) Birria Mother Recipe No. 1 (page 15)

2 cups (280 g) Mexipoix (page 147)

Roasted Poblano Sauce (page 37), for drizzling

1. Heat a griddle to 375ºF (190ºC).

2. Add the oil to the griddle surface and spread it around a bit with a spatula. Place the hot dogs on the griddle in the oil. Rotate the hot dogs back and forth so they get evenly coated with the oil. Cook until all sides are equally bronzed, 7 to 10 minutes.

3. Meanwhile, prepare the cheese blanket by spreading ⅓-cup (40 g) mounds of shredded cheese on the hot griddle (you should have 6 total).

4. While the cheese is melting and the hot dogs are cooking, toast the inside of the hot dog buns by opening and placing inside down on the cooking surface.

5. When the cheese begins to form a thin crust and the top side is melty (at about 2 minutes), scrape it off, open a hot dog bun, and place the cheese blanket in the center. Repeat with the remaining cheese and buns.

6. The hot dog should be ready at this point, so place it in the middle of the cheese blanket.

7. Top the hot dog with about a ⅓ cup (80 g) of birria, a generous amount of Mexipoix, and a healthy drizzle of the roasted poblano sauce. Serve.

CHAPTER 5

Dishes with a Birria Base 2: Global Fusion

BIRRIA GYOZAS WITH NUOC CHAM

My amazing partner, Audrey, and I own a food business in Nashville called Secret Bodega. We started off doing pop-ups, and the very first one was a collab with the maestro himself, Julio Hernandez of Maíz de la Vida. We had made a bunch of birria gyozas to show off how creative we were, but like a bunch of rookies we let them half thaw from frozen, then placed them in the freezer again so they all stuck together, essentially destroying most of them. We were able to salvage a few, and the ones we did were magical. Let that be a lesson to you: Keep your gyozas frozen at all times before cooking.

    P.S. I've included the nuoc cham recipe we used as a dipping sauce for the gyozas that our friend JP Murphy shared with us. The flavors all danced nicely on our tongues, and it is a nice change from just using consommé for a dipping sauce.

MAKES 40 gyozas

2½ cups (600 g) Birria Mother Recipe No. 1 (page 15), patted dry

½ cup (70 g) Mexipoix (page 147)

40 gyoza wrappers or round wonton wrappers

1 tablespoon (15 ml) sesame oil

1 cup (240 ml) water

1 tablespoon (8 g) flour

1. In a large bowl, combine the birria and Mexipoix. Using your hands, mix well.

2. Place 1 tablespoon (15 g) of filling in the middle of a dumpling wrapper. Using your finger, lightly wet the half of the outer rim with water. Fold the wrapper in half. Using your fingertips, make pleats to seal the dumpling. Repeat with the remaining wrappers and filling.

3. In a large nonstick skillet, heat the sesame oil over medium heat. Add half of the dumplings in a circle. Fry for 1 to 3 minutes, until the side down is slightly browned.

4. Pour a ¼ cup (60 ml) of water directly into the pan and cover. Lower heat and steam the dumplings until the water has mostly evaporated, 6 to 7 minutes. Remove the lid and continue cooking until the water has completely evaporated.

5. Place a plate on top of the filled dumplings. Flip the pan upside down while pressing the plate to invert the dumplings. Cook the remaining dumplings.

6. Serve with nuoc cham dipping sauce.

(continued)

NUOC CHAM

6 tablespoons (90 ml) warm water

2 tablespoons (26 g) sugar

1½ tablespoons (23 ml) freshly squeezed lime juice

2 tablespoons (30 ml) fish sauce

1 clove garlic, minced

1 Thai chile, thinly sliced

1. Combine water and sugar in a bowl. Stir. Let cool.

2. Add lime juice and fish sauce. Stir until combined.

3. Top with garlic and chiles.

"TRADITIONAL" BIRRIA RAMEN

I've seen very high-end ramen shops make versions of birria ramen and usually feel that they're just trying too hard. I'm not knocking their high-end creations, but in my opinion birria ramen was probably originally created with leftover birria after a night of drinking. For this reason, I think it should be approachable, and that's what I've tried to do with this recipe. It calls for the ramen you subsisted on through college. I used the Tapatío brand of ramen because I like their spice packet more than the other brands, but feel free to use what you prefer.

SERVES 1

One 3.8-ounce (108 g) cup instant ramen

2 cups (480 ml) Birria Consommé (page 28)

½ cup (120 g) Birria Mother Recipe No. 1 (page 15), reheated

Mexipoix (page 147)

1 soft-boiled egg

Lime wedges, for serving

1. In a medium bowl, add the ramen noodles with the birria consommé. Let the ramen noodles cook and get soft, about 3 minutes.

2. Add the spice pack and stir until well combined.

3. Top with birria, Mexipoix, and the perfectly cooked egg. Add a squeeze from a juicy lime. Enjoy!

SPICY BEEF BIRRIA RAMEN

This is how you turn that sad pack of ramen noodles into the best thirty-three-cent investment you've ever made.

SERVES 1

One 3-ounce (85 g) package instant ramen, spice pack discarded

2 cups (480 ml) Birria Consommé (page 28)

½ cup (120 g) Spicy Beef Birria (page 27), reheated

½ large, fresh jalapeño, thinly sliced

1 radish, thinly sliced

Crushed pork rinds

Chopped cilantro

Finely chopped onion

Lime wedges, for serving

1. Place the ramen in a bowl and cover with the birria consommé.

2. Let the ramen noodles cook and get soft, about 3 minutes, before stirring.

3. Stir. Top with birria, jalapeño slices, radish slices, pork rinds, cilantro, and onion. Serve with lime wedges for squeezing.

4. Sit back and watch your friends hail you as a culinary god.

BIRRIA YAKI ONIGIRI

I visited Japan a few years back and fell in love with their bodega food culture. I also became obsessed with onigiri as it became my constant snack throughout my visit. One of my favorite memories was scarfing down multiple onigiri on the bullet train through the Japanese countryside. Not too long ago I had yaki onigiri at Kisser, one of my favorite restaurants in Nashville. This inspired me to combine my love for birria and for that onigiri I've never stopped thinking about.

SERVES 12

2 cups (390 g) sushi rice

1 teaspoon kosher salt

¼ cup (60 g) Birria Mother Recipe No. 1 (page 15), finely shredded and completely drained

3 cups (720 ml) Birria Consommé (page 28)

MAKE THE SUSHI RICE

1. Place the sushi rice in a large bowl and add water to 2 inches (5 cm) above rice. Gently swish around with your hands to rinse, then drain. Repeat the process until water is almost clear (about three more times).

2. Pour cold water over the rice until 1 inch (2.5 cm) above the rice and let soak for 30 minutes. Pour through a fine-mesh sieve.

3. Combine the rice and 2½ cups (600 ml) of water in a medium saucepan and bring to a boil over high heat, stirring occasionally.

4. Reduce heat to low, cover, and simmer the rice until the water is absorbed, 12 to 14 minutes.

5. Remove from the heat and let sit covered for 15 minutes, allowing the rice to steam and become tender.

6. Uncover and gently fluff the rice with a fork. Let sit until cool enough to handle, about 10 minutes.

MAKE THE ONIGIRI

1. Fill a small bowl with tap water, and add 1 teaspoon of kosher salt.

2. Dip your hands in the salted water, then scoop a little less than ⅓ cup (80 g) of the sushi rice into your hand and form into a thick disk, 3 to 4 inches (7.5 to 10 cm) in diameter. Keep the remaining rice in the pot covered.

3. Create a small indentation in the center and add 2 teaspoons of birria.

(continued)

4. Use your hands to carefully shape the rice and push it over the birria to create a sphere (birria should not be visible), then press firmly between your index finger and thumb while using your palms to form the rice into a triangle.

5. Set the triangle aside on a cutting board and repeat with the remaining rice and birria, dipping your hands in the salt water mixture between each triangle.

6. In a medium frying pan, add enough oil to coat the bottom. Heat over medium-high heat until shimmering.

7. Place the triangles in the pan and sear until brown and crispy for 2 to 3 minutes. Flip and sear the other side.

8. Serve with a side of consommé for dipping.

BIRRIA GOULASH WITH KALE SALAD

My friend Aaron Clemins runs what is quite possibly the best sandwich shop in Nashville, Bill's Sandwich Palace. The magic that he creates in between two slices of bread is nothing short of amazing. We are both sandwich fanatics, but what we really bonded over was our love and fond memories of hearty Midwestern food. Aaron and I have formed a great friendship, and when I invited him to share a recipe for this book, I made the poor assumption that he would be creating a sandwich, but what I got instead was a big, hearty Midwest hug of a dish and I couldn't have been happier.

SERVES 4 to 6

SPAETZLE

¾ cup (180 ml) whole milk

¾ cup (180 ml) water

2 cups (250 g) all-purpose flour

1 cup (128 g) rye flour

2 teaspoons kosher salt, plus more for boiling

Neutral oil, such as sunflower or vegetable

4 tablespoons (55 g) unsalted butter, divided

MAKE THE SPAETZLE

1. In a medium bowl, whisk together the milk and water, then add the all-purpose flour, rye flour, and salt and mix together with a rubber spatula. Mix until a smooth batter forms and there are no lumps. Cover with plastic wrap and refrigerate for 30 minutes.

2. Meanwhile, bring 6 quarts (5.4 L) of water to a gentle boil with 2 tablespoons (30 g) of salt.

3. Set a colander on the pot and, working in small batches, scoop and push the batter through the holes in the boiling water. Cook for 2 to 3 minutes and scoop out onto a small cookie sheet or mixing bowl using a slotted spoon.

4. When all the spaetzle are cooked, toss with a small amount of neutral oil to prevent them from sticking together.

5. Heat 1 tablespoon (14 g) of the butter in a large nonstick skillet. Once it foams, add a quarter of the spaetzle and cook, 4 to 6 minutes, tossing every few moments to ensure even browning, and add to a serving bowl. Repeat with the remaining spaetzle.

(continued)

KALE SALAD

2 bunches kale, finely chopped

¼ cup (60 ml) extra-virgin olive oil

1½ tablespoons (23 ml) lemon juice

Pinch of kosher salt

TO SERVE

3 cups (720 g) beef birria

⅓ cup (40 g) shredded Parmigiano-
Reggiano

¼ cup (25 g) toasted breadcrumbs or
crushed croutons

MAKE THE KALE SALAD

1. Chop the kale and dress with your desired amount of olive oil, lemon juice, and salt.

SERVE

1. Spoon the birria over the spaetzle and top with kale salad, grated cheese, and breadcrumbs.

BIRRITALIAN BEEF

Italian beef in Chicago is so dominant as a local dish that it doesn't occur to the born-and-raised Chicagoans that it's not available everywhere. I grew up with my mom and aunts, who loved traveling to extended family weddings, saving cousins a bit of cash on catering all the while laying a base for receptions that were reliably wild.

I just didn't know it wasn't the same for everyone else. My personal *Twilight Zone* moment happened during my first week of college in the South. I was just making casual conversation like you would about the weather or sports.

Me: "What's a good place to get Italian beef around here?"

Nice, unassuming person: ". . . Italian beef? You mean like a roast beef sandwich?"

Me: *Screams in Dennis Farina accent.*

Part of the horror is the existential feeling of opportunity loss. French dip is NOT the same as an Italian beef, and any such implication is showing your lack of familiarity. There's magic to a just-soaked in au jus beef that sets this apart from anything else in the world.

But WAIT! This isn't about being provincial. It's about how Italian beef, the *ethos*, translates so well that none of us Chicago meatballs can conceive of it not existing elsewhere. So please enjoy this marriage of birria and Italian beef, a creation of John Carruthers. It works so well, so naturally, that it feels less like tasting a culinary crossover than it does finding $20 in a jeans pocket on laundry day.

Go get that twenty.

SERVES 8

STOCK

7 pounds (3.2 kg) beef bones from marrow, shanks, or oxtail

4 tablespoons (64 g) double-concentrated tomato paste

Flour, for dusting

5 white onions, chopped

1 celery rib, chopped, leaves removed

4 carrots, peeled and chopped

4 dried ancho chiles, stems removed

6 dried cascabel chiles, stems removed

2 bay leaves

¼ teaspoon Ceylon cinnamon

1 tablespoon (3 g) fresh thyme leaves

1 tablespoon (3 g) chopped parsley, roots only

1 tablespoon (10 g) black peppercorns

MAKE THE STOCK

1. Preheat the oven to 325ºF (170ºC).

2. Rinse and dry the beef bones. Rub with the tomato paste, then dust with flour. Transfer to a sheet pan, taking care to shake off any excess flour. Roast until well browned, about 30 minutes.

3. Meanwhile, add the vegetables to a sheet pan and roast until tender, about 30 minutes.

4. Heat a small skillet over medium-high heat. Toast the chiles in the dry pan until just fragrant and pliable, about 5 minutes.

(continued)

PASTE

12 ounces (340 g) beef tallow, room temperature, whipped

2 tablespoons (38 g) kosher salt

2 slices smoked bacon, diced

4 cloves garlic

2 tablespoons (16 g) ancho chile powder

1 tablespoon (8 g) cascabel chile powder

1 teaspoon Mexican oregano

½ teaspoon dried ground thyme

1 tablespoon (4 g) chopped parsley

2 teaspoons black pepper

Olive oil (optional)

4 pounds (1.8 kg) top or bottom round

Bolillo buns (or, failing that, telera rolls. Or I'm not your dad, use hot dog buns for all I care)

5. Transfer the bones and vegetables to a large stockpot and cover with cold water. Add the chiles, bay leaves, cinnamon, thyme, parsley ends, and peppercorns and bring to a low simmer over low heat. If you see a little bubble action, you're doing it right. Rock that same lazy simmer for 8 to 12 hours.

6. Pour the stock through a fine-mesh strainer into another large pot or bowl. The stock is now ready to store or use. To store, transfer to an airtight container and keep refrigerated for up to 7 days.

MAKE THE PASTE

1. Place everything in a food processor and process until a smooth, thick paste forms. If the ingredients will not blend, add olive oil 1 teaspoon at a time.

MAKE THE BEEF

1. Rub the beef with every bit of the paste. Does it seem like too much? Perfect, then you've added just the right amount. Transfer to a wire rack set over a sheet pan. Cover and refrigerate overnight.

2. Preheat the oven to 325ºF (170ºC).

3. Transfer the rack and meat to a roasting pan and cook for 1 hour, then remove the rack, pour in the stock, and braise for 1 more hour. When it is a perfect medium-rare (130ºF [54ºC]), remove, cool, and refrigerate overnight.

4. Remove the cooled beef from the liquid and slice as thin as possible. If you want the real deal, you need a meat slicer that's up to the task. A good slicer will cut the meat so thin that you can read a newspaper through a slice.

5. Gently heat the reserved cooking liquid to just steaming in a medium pot over low heat.

6. Add the thin-sliced beef to the steaming stock. Cook until warmed through, about 30 minutes.

7. Fish the meat out and divide it equally between the buns. Firmly grip the bun with tongs and dunk it briefly in and out of the stock a few times. The bread will be soggy but not falling apart. Think baptism, but not the born-again adult kind.

8. Place a piece of foil on top of a piece of parchment paper, shiny side up.

9. Slap the juicy sandwich onto the bottom corner of the overlaid paper and foil, and roll tightly.

10. Just let it hang out a minute. This is where the final magic occurs. Equilibrium, osmosis, or just cosmic understanding. Unwrap and enjoy.

SOUS VIDE RACK OF LAMB AND FRITES

JP Murphy and I had an instant connection when we first met, which led to us being roommates when I moved to Nashville from Chicago. JP has an impressive and extensive culinary background. He runs Cabin Attic Burgers and makes THE best damn fries I've ever had. I encouraged him to go back to his fancy food roots for this recipe and he obliged. You will need sous vide equipment for this recipe, along with time and patience. The results are extraordinary.

JP had very specific instructions for this dish: "Spoon and swipe the white sauce on one side of the plate. Following the same pattern, spoon and swipe the red sauce directly on top of the white. Pile your frites in a large pile so they are very tall, then carefully lean your lamb cuts, exposing the perfect cook, against your tower of frites."

Do as the chef does.

SERVES 4

SOUS VIDE LAMB

1 rack of lamb

1 teaspoon black peppercorns

¼ teaspoon cumin seeds

1 dried Anaheim chile, destemmed, deseeded

2 dried guajillo chiles

2 dried chiles de árbol, destemmed, deseeded

1 bay leaf

5 cloves garlic, crushed

½ cup (8 g) chopped cilantro

1 tablespoon (12 g) tomato salt (50/50 mix of tomato powder and kosher salt)

1 tablespoon (15 g) gochujang

½ Vidalia onion, diced

Birria Starter (page 29)

MAKE THE LAMB

1. Set up the immersion circulator and water bath. Set the immersion circulator to 130°F (54.5°F).

2. Cut away the fat between the bones and scrape away the sinew with a knife. In a small sauté pan set over medium-high heat, add the black peppercorns and cumin seeds. Toss constantly until fragrant, about 7 minutes. Transfer to a small bowl and set aside.

3. Place the Anaheim, guajillo, and árbol chiles in the sauté pan and reduce the heat to medium. Allow each side of the chiles to cook for 3 minutes and then flip and cook until fragrant and dark, about 2 more minutes. In a vacuum sealer bag, place the black peppercorns, cumin seeds, toasted chiles, bay leaf, garlic, and cilantro.

4. Pat the rack of lamb dry, then salt thoroughly with the tomato salt and sprinkle generously with the gochujang. Place the seasoned rack of lamb in the vacuum sealer bag and vacuum and seal the bag. If you don't have a vacuum sealer, you can use a large zip-top plastic bag. Make sure to remove the air by leaving a crack in the seal as you submerge it in the water bath. Be sure to seal it before fully submerging it.

(continued)

POMMES FRITES

2 russet potatoes

4 quarts (3.6 L) peanut oil

Salt, to taste

Queso fresco (optional)

WHITE SAUCE

1 cup (230 g) crema or sour cream

1 lime, zested and juiced

RED SAUCE

1 quart (960 ml) Birria Starter (page 29)

5. Place the vacuum-sealed bag in a water bath and cook for 2 hours. After 2 hours, remove the vacuum-sealed bag from the water bath and place in an ice bath for 15 minutes.

6. Heat a large sauté pan over high heat. Take a dollop of the fat on top of the birria starter and throw it in the pan. Sear the rack of lamb for a total of 4 minutes, making sure you flip and rotate it in the pan to create a good sear on all the sides of the meat. Place on a rack to cool for 2 minutes before slicing.

MAKE THE POMMES FRITES

1. Peel the potatoes. Place them in an ice bath immediately after peeling to prevent browning.

2. Cut the potatoes into long ½-inch (1.3 cm)-wide sticks and soak in an ice bath for a minimum of 30 minutes and a maximum of 12 hours.

3. Pour the oil into a large Dutch oven and heat to 275°F (140°C). Remove the potatoes from their ice bath and place on a tea towel. Pat dry.

4. Working in batches, gently place the potatoes in the heated oil and cook until brown and crispy, about 6 minutes.

5. Remove from the oil and place on a rack over a sheet pan to allow the excess oil to drain and cool. Transfer the cooked fries to the refrigerator to completely cool. They can be stored for up to 2 days in a sheet pan or open bowl.

6. Just before serving, heat up the oil in the Dutch oven to 375ºF (190ºC). Working in batches and using a deep-fryer sieve, gently place the cold french fries in the hot oil. Cook for 3 minutes. They should be a deep, golden brown color.

7. Place a kitchen towel in a large bowl and add the hot french fries. Remove the towel and sprinkle salt and queso fresco on the french fries. Toss to combine.

MAKE THE WHITE SAUCE

1. Thoroughly mix the crema, lime juice, and lime zest together.

MAKE THE RED SAUCE

1. After making the birria base, allow it to cool so the fat separates and rises to the top. Remove the fat cap off the birria base.

2. In a large sauté pan over high heat, reduce the birria base liquid until it is thick enough to coat the back of a spoon.

CHICAGO TAVERN–STYLE BIRRIA PIZZA

John Carruthers is many things: my former writing partner (we've written two cookbooks together), one of my best friends, and a brilliant food mind. John's obsession is Chicago tavern–style pizza, which he has absolutely perfected and it's been such a marvel to watch. We're now a few states away from each other, but when we get together in the kitchen, it's muscle memory—we flow and create like we're still in our tiny test kitchen in Chicago.

John invited me to come up to Chicago for a pizza collab with him and our other BFF, John Scholl. I had previously done a birria pizza with my friends Ashley and Ryan in Colorado with their outfit, Outside Pizza, and it was a great hit. Outside Pizza is a beautifully crafted Neapolitan-style pizza, which is vastly different from thin crust, tavern-style pizza, so I was excited at the prospect of making birria pizza in the style that I grew up eating.

John graciously let me share his pizza recipe, which I admittingly dream about. The star of the show is the cracker-thin crust that belongs on display at the pizza version of the Louvre. For our collab we skipped the sauce and mixed the mozzarella with Chihuahua cheese because cheese can always be cheesier.

MAKES 1 pizza

CRUST

3 cups (365 g) high-gluten flour

4 teaspoons (13 g) cornmeal

1¼ teaspoons sugar

1 teaspoon salt

½ teaspoon instant yeast

¾ cup (180 ml) ice-cold water (35°F [2°C])

2 tablespoons (30 ml) olive oil, plus more to store

TOPPING

1⅓ cups (150 g) shredded full-fat low-moisture mozzarella

½ cup (60 g) shredded Chihuahua cheese

1 cup (240 g) Birria Mother Recipe No. 1 (page 15), moist but not wet

Mexipoix (page 147)

Roasted Poblano Sauce (page 37), in a squeeze bottle

MAKE THE CRUST

1. Add the dry ingredients to the bowl of a food processor fitted with a dough blade and pulse to combine.

2. Clear the sides of the processor bowl with a spatula and pour in the oil and water along the sides.

3. Process until the dough begins to cohere and runs above the blade. Count to 30, then stop the processor and set aside for 20 minutes.

4. Free the dough from the blade and process again for 40 seconds.

5. Remove the dough and form into a ball. Divide the dough into 2 equal balls roughly 10 ounces (280 g) each.

6. Oil the balls lightly and place each into a 32-ounce (960 g) deli container. Close the lid and label with the date.

7. Ferment the dough in the fridge for a minimum of 12 hours and a maximum of 10 days.

(continued)

8. The night before you make the pizza, remove the dough from the fridge and let warm to room temperature for 2 to 3 hours. Then roll out the dough to a 14-inch (35.5 cm) round and dock on both sides with a fork or dough docker. Store the rolled and docked sheets between sheets of nonstick parchment and keep in the fridge overnight, uncovered. A pan under the stack will make it easier to move in and out of the fridge. This is called "curing," and it's the difference between a pretty good tavern-style pizza and a fantastic one. If you go past 24 hours of curing, the dough will begin to get brittle and curl. So only cure if you're looking to bake the next day.

ADD THE TOPPING AND BAKE

NOTE: For this step, John insists you use a pizza steel, which is pretty easy to find these days. I like a 16-inch (40.5 cm) steel at $^3/_8$-inch (1 cm) thickness, but a 14-inch (35.5 cm) at the same thickness also leads to a good result.

1. Preheat the oven to 550°F (290°C) for 1 hour.

2. Lightly dust a wooden peel with cornmeal. Turn the dough off of the paper directly onto the peel and dock it again if there's still some moisture.

3. In a small bowl, combine the mozzarella and Chihuahua cheese and spread across the pizza to the edges. Evenly spread the birria on top of the cheese. Launch the pizza onto the steel and cook undisturbed for 8 minutes.

4. After 8 minutes, use a metal peel or spatula to rotate the pizza for any uneven cooking and to check the bottom for doneness. If not cooked through, return to the oven for up to 4 more minutes. The cheese should be well baked.

5. Remove from the oven, spread your desired Mexipoix across the pizza, and finish by adding a medium-thick swirl of the roasted poblano sauce, starting from the center and working your way to the edge of the pizza. Let cool 1 to 2 minutes.

6. Transfer the pizza to a cutting board and slice. For a true Chicago-style, cut into 3 x 3-inch (8 x 9 cm) squares.

TAMPA BAY CUBANO CON BIRRIA

The origins of the Cuban sandwich will forever be debated. My buddy Marco Reyna insists that it was originally created in Tampa Bay (the area where he conveniently resides in and where his brewery, Home State Brewing Co., is located in). Leave it to two Mexicans from Chicago to discuss the history of the Cuban sandwich in Florida and come up with a Mexican version of it.

MAKES 2 sandwiches

Two 12-inch (30.5 cm) Cuban sandwich loaves or French bread

Yellow mustard

12 ounces (340 g) Pork Birria (page 24)

4 ounces (115 g) baked ham, thinly sliced

5 ounces (140 g) Genoa salami

4 ounces (115 g) Swiss cheese

12 spicy pickle slices

Butter or beef fat

Birria Consommé (page 28), for dipping (optional)

1. Cut the bread into four 8-inch (20 cm) pieces and slice lengthwise.

2. Spread mustard on the top half of each sandwich.

3. To assemble the sandwiches, layer the birria followed by slices of ham, salami, Swiss cheese, and pickles.

4. Butter the outside of the bread or use the birria starter (beef) fat. Use a panini press or cast-iron skillet with a hefty weight to cook the sandwiches until the cheese is melted and the bread is golden brown, about 4 minutes each side.

5. Cut the sandwich in half at a 45-degree angle and serve with hot consommé, if desired.

PRO TIP: Look for bread with a thinner crust so that as it presses, the outside remains crisp but the juices from the birria don't seep through and make the sandwich soggy.

BIRRIA PIEROGIES

Chicago has a very large Polish population, so there was never a shortage of solid Polish food at my disposal. When I moved to Nashville, I started getting some pretty disturbing cravings for pierogies and none of the horrible frozen options at the local chain grocery store would suffice. Wouldn't you know it, there's a dude in Nashville from Upstate New York making Polish-style pierogies. My pal Derek Shampine, chef/owner of Upstate Pierogi Co., was the answer to my Polish prayers! This recipe is my homage to Derek and the Polish pierogies from Chicago that I so missed.

MAKES 20 pierogies

PIEROGI DOUGH

2 cups (250 g) flour

Pinch of salt

¼ cup (55 g) butter, melted

½ cup (115 g) sour cream

1 large egg

FILLING

1 cup (240 g) leftover mashed potatoes

1 cup (120 g) grated Chihuahua cheese

1 cup (240 g) Birria Mother Recipe No. 1 (page 15)

TO COOK

1 tablespoon (14 g) beef fat

TO SERVE

Chipotle Crema (page 44)

Birria Consommé (page 28), hot (optional)

MAKE THE DOUGH

1. Mix the flour and salt in a large bowl. Stir in the melted butter, sour cream, and egg. Stir until somewhat combined, then knead with your hands until smooth. Be careful not to overwork the dough. Wrap and refrigerate for at least 30 minutes.

MAKE THE FILLING AND ASSEMBLE

1. In a large bowl, stir together the potatoes, cheese, and birria.

2. Roll the dough until it is about ⅛ inch (3 mm) thick. Cut out rounds about 3 inches (7.5 cm) in diameter.

3. Place 1½ tablespoons (23 g) of the filling onto a dough round and use your finger to rub a small amount of water on the edge of the dough. Fold the dough over the filling, forming a semicircle. Pinch the edges to seal. Repeat with the remaining dough and filling.

4. Bring a large pot of salted water to a boil and carefully add the pierogis and cook until they float, 3 to 5 minutes.

5. Heat the beef fat in a large skillet over high heat. Add the pierogi in a single layer. Do not overcrowd. You may need to work in batches. Cook for 2 to 3 minutes per side until evenly browned. Remove from the heat.

6. Plate the pierogi and spread chipotle crema across the top. If you're feeling frisky, dip the pierogi in hot consommé.

BIRRIA CROISSANTS

Hannah Yoon makes the best croissants I have ever had. They're soft, buttery, and perfect on their own, but not leaving well enough alone, I knew we could make the best even better. Hannah has been making a split-top croissant filled with whatever deliciousness she picks each week. I somehow convinced her to share her recipe, and we filled the split top with birria and melty cheese. A win-win. This recipe takes patience and time, but it is so well worth it and completely satisfying when you're indulging in this fine creation.

MAKES 12 croissants

DOUGH

1¾ cups (420 ml) water

1 cup (240 ml) whole milk

¾ ounce (20 g) active sourdough starter (100% hydration)

10 cups (1.2 kg) all-purpose or bread flour

⅔ cup (130 g) granulated sugar

1½ tablespoons (23 g) kosher salt

2 teaspoons (12 g) dry yeast

7 tablespoons (100 g) unsalted butter, cubed

BUTTER BLOCK

1 pound (454 g) 83% European butter

EGG WASH

2 or 3 large eggs

Milk (optional)

FILLING

3 cups (720 g) beef birria

2 cups (240 g) shredded Chihuahua cheese

TO SERVE

Birria Consommé (page 28), hot

MAKE THE DOUGH

1. In a stand mixer with a dough hook, mix all the ingredients for the dough except the cubed butter, starting with the wet ingredients first.

2. When the dough has roughly come together in the mixer, add the cubed butter piece by piece and let mix until the dough is homogenized and does not stick to the sides of the bowl. Take the dough out of the mixer and shape into a flat rectangle roughly the size of a half sheet pan, 13 x 18 inches (33 x 45 cm).

3. Stick the dough "block" into the freezer to set overnight.

ADD THE BUTTER BLOCK

1. Add the European butter to a stand mixer with a paddle. Paddle the butter until soft enough to mold with your hands and you feel no remaining chunks. The butter should be pliable but not aerated.

2. Take the butter out of the mixing bowl and shape into a flat rectangle roughly the size of a quarter sheet pan, 13 x 9 inches (33 x 23 cm).

3. Stick the butter "block" into the refrigerator to set overnight.

(continued)

LAMINATE THE DOUGH

1. Pull the dough block out of the freezer and let it come up to temperature (should still be cold to the touch but not frozen).

2. Pull the butter block out of the fridge and let it come up to temperature (should be flexible without getting melty or shiny).

3. When both the dough and butter blocks are the appropriate temperatures, roughly fit the butter block evenly on one side of the dough block. Make sure all the corners are lined up. Then fold the other half of the dough block over the top side of the butter block (this should roughly look like a book with butter on the inside).

4. Take a sharp blade or paring knife and split the seam of the dough block. This will alleviate pressure when you start to laminate.

5. Start to roll out the block with the "seam" facing to the right. Roll out to 12 inches (30 cm). Then rotate the block 90 degrees so the seam is facing up. Then roll out the length of the block to 36 inches (91 cm). When the dough block is at the appropriate height and length, fold the end of the block one-third of the way in, and fold the other third on top of it. (It should look like a piece of paper folded three ways to fit inside an envelope.) The seam should still be facing up.

6. Rotate the block another 90 degrees so the seam is facing to the right again and begin to roll out the block. Roll out to 12 inches (30 cm). Then rotate the block 90 degrees so the seam is facing up. Then roll out the length of the block to 36 inches (91 cm).

7. Fold the ends of the block into itself in another tri-fold and put the now laminated dough block into the refrigerator to rest for at least 3 or 4 hours.

SHAPE THE CROISSANTS

1. Once the dough block has had time to rest in the fridge, you can now roll it out and begin to shape. Similar to the first steps of lamination, roll out the height of the block to 12 inches (30 cm), rotate the block 90 degrees, and roll out the length of the block to 36 inches (91 cm). When rolling out to shape, it is important that you are checking the thickness of the final roll.

2. Roll the long sheet of dough onto a rolling pin to pick up, then roll out onto a clean flat surface to begin to cut and shape. Cut triangle croissants, making sure the base of the triangle is 4 inches (10 cm) long and the height is 12 inches (30 cm).

3. Take the base of the triangle and begin to roll it up into itself all the way to the tip of the triangle. It should now look like a very small croissant!

4. Continue to shape and roll the remainder of the dough block until you have 12 croissants.

PROOF THE CROISSANTS

1. Place the croissants equidistant apart on a baking sheet. Make sure you give them each enough space in between as you begin the proofing process. Place the baking sheet in a warm area to proof.

2. Once you see that each layer is distinguishably puffy and is starting to "split," the croissants are properly proofed and ready to start baking. Another good indicator is that each croissant jiggles gently if jiggling the entire tray.

BRUSH WITH EGG WASH AND BAKE

1. Preheat the oven to 450°F (230°C). Put an extra baking sheet on the bottom of the oven to act as a steam riser and preheat with the oven.

2. In a bowl, whisk the eggs until they are fully homogenized. You can also add milk or any other kind of fat to mix into the egg wash. With a pastry brush, brush the egg wash onto the proofed croissant shapes.

3. When the oven is up to temperature, pour a bit of water onto the baking sheet you've been preheating in the oven and put the croissants into the oven to bake.

4. Bake for about 15 minutes or until the outside of the croissants have evenly browned to your liking. Remove from the oven and let cool.

ADD THE BIRRIA FILLING

1. Preheat the oven to 350°F (180°C).

2. Split the croissants down the center with a serrated knife, but don't cut all the way through to the bottom. Fill the inside with birria and top with cheese.

3. Place the filled croissants on a baking sheet and bake for about 10 minutes or until the cheese has fully melted and the birria inside is hot.

4. Serve with a side of consommé. You can either drizzle it on top or dip the croissant to your liking.

CRUNCH WRAPS

Crunch wraps will never be accused of being an authentic Mexican snack, but that doesn't take away how fun they are to make and eat. My partner Audrey added this to our arsenal of offerings for our food pop-ups around town and it's quickly become a favorite.

PRO TIP: You can substitute the tostada in this recipe for your favorite Doritos for an extra layer of fun flavor. Your inner stoner will thank you for that.

MAKES 4 wraps

1 tablespoon (15 ml) vegetable oil

1 cup (240 g) **Pressure Cooker Refried Beans (page 146)**

4 **Flour Tortillas (page 135)**

1 cup (160 g) **chopped tomatoes**

2 cups (70 g) **shredded lettuce**

4 **tostada shells**

1 cup (240 ml) **Mexican crema**

2 cups (480 g) **Birria Mother Recipe No. 1 (page 15), hot**

½ cup (120 ml) **Cerveza Cheese (page 43)**

1 cup (120 g) **shredded cheddar cheese**

1 cup (120 g) **shredded Chihuahua cheese**

1. Heat a large nonstick skillet over medium heat, then add the vegetable oil.

2. Add a ¼ cup (60 g) of the refried beans to the center of each tortilla, leaving a generous border for folding.

3. Add ¼ cup (40 g) of the tomatoes on top of the beans, followed by ½ cup (18 g) of the shredded lettuce.

4. Place a tostada on top of the lettuce, followed by ¼ cup (60 ml) of the crema and ½ cup (120 g) of the birria.

5. Drizzle 2 tablespoons (30 ml) of the cerveza cheese over the birria, then top that with ¼ cup (60 g) of the cheddar cheese and ¼ cup (60 g) of the Chihuahua cheese.

6. Tightly fold the edges of the tortilla toward the center, creating pleats. Quickly invert the crunch wrap so the pleats are on the bottom and they stay together.

7. Add the crunch wraps, seam side down, to the skillet and cook until the tortilla is golden, about 3 minutes per side. Repeat with the remaining crunch wraps.

CHAPTER 6

Classic Birria Main Courses

QUESABIRRIA TACOS

Whereas traditional birria was a peasant dish born in the homes in the Mexican state of Jalisco centuries ago, quesabirria tacos were born on the streets of Tijuana, Mexico, less than twenty years ago. Birria tacos were never the staple at taco restaurants that they have since become: It's believed that street taco vendors and food trucks began making birria tacos around 2009, adding quesadilla cheese for an upcharge upon request. Around 2016 is when Tijuana taco vendors, *taqueros*, brought their cheese-smothered creations to Los Angeles—because it's simply a fact that the best way to turn humble birria into a flavor party is by covering it in a bunch of melted cheese.

This is your official invitation to that party. We're going to teach you how to make quesabirria at home.

MAKES 4 tacos

1 heaping cup (240 g) Birria Mother Recipe No. 1 (page 15), shredded and reheated

4 corn tortillas

¼ cup (60 g) birria fat or vegetable oil

1 cup (120 g) shredded Mexican quesadilla cheese

Mexipoix (page 147)

1. In a small bowl, set aside the shredded birria meat, making sure to add some of the birria broth so the meat isn't dry.

2. Heat a large nonstick or cast-iron skillet over medium heat.

3. Dip one side of each tortilla into the birria fat, then place in the hot pan, fat side down.

4. Let the tortillas begin to sizzle, then sprinkle ¼ cup (30 g) of cheese and ¼ cup (60 g) of meat over half of each tortilla.

5. As the tortillas brown and the cheese starts to melt, fold each tortilla in half to cover the meat, pressing down gently.

6. Flip the tortillas as needed to avoid burning. Cook until crisp on both sides.

7. Before you're ready to bite into the tacos, slightly open them and add your Mexipoix to each one.

BIRRIA TORTAS

Truth be told, I will take a torta over a taco any day. So naturally when my birria obsession began, I had to go out and buy some bolillos to make a birria torta at home. This is better than any store-bought torta, and pretty soon you'll be picking tortas over tacos when you visit your favorite Mexican food joint.

SERVES 4 tortas

4 telera or bolillo rolls

2 tablespoons (28 g) butter, softened

2 cups (480 g) Birria Mother Recipe No. 1 (page 15)

Mexican crema or sour cream

¼ cup (60 g) Pressure Cooker Refried Beans (page 146)

Finely shredded iceberg lettuce

2 avocados, sliced

12 thin slices tomato

Escabeche (page 49)

Habanero Salsa (page 42)

1. Split the telera or bolillo rolls in half. If the bolillos are large, remove the bread filling so you're left with 2 medium-thin slices of bread. Butter the inside of each piece.

2. In a large skillet over medium-high heat, place the rolls, buttered side down, toasting the buns until they are golden. Transfer to a plate and cover with a tea towel.

3. Add the birria to the skillet and cook, stirring often, until warmed through, about 5 minutes.

4. Slather the inside top piece of bread with the Mexican crema.

5. Build the torta: beans on the bottom bun, followed by the birria, lettuce, then the avocado and tomato.

6. Top with escabeche and salsa for extra flavor.

ENCHILADAS NORTENAS CON BIRRIA

My mom makes THE best enchiladas I have ever had. When I return to Chicago to visit her, enchiladas are the one dish I absolutely have to have. We're now a few states apart, so I had to try my best to make my own delicious enchiladas to hold me over until I can have hers again.

MAKES 12 enchiladas

Canola oil

2 cups (240 g) shredded Chihuahua cheese

1 cup (120 g) crumbled queso fresco

1 cup (16 g) finely chopped cilantro

¾ cup (120 g) finely chopped red onion

1 cup (240 g) Birria Mother Recipe No. 1 (page 15)

3 cups (720 ml) Classic Adobo (page 32)

12 corn tortillas

Mexican crema

1. Add a thin layer of oil to a frying pan and heat over medium-low until shimmering.

2. Meanwhile, in a medium bowl, toss the Chihuahua cheese and crumbled queso fresco with the cilantro and red onion.

3. Evenly mix the birria into the adobo in a shallow, wide bowl.

4. Place a tortilla on top of the birria mixture, then flip, evenly coating both sides. Set the tortilla in the frying pan, cook for 10 seconds, flip, and add ¼ cup (30 g) of the cheese mixture and some birria across and toward the top of the tortilla, leaving a little "lip" of tortilla. Using two spatulas, roll the enchilada, covering the cheese and birria filling.

5. Cook for 2 minutes until the sauce gets thick and tacky, then carefully turn over and cook for another 2 minutes or until the cheese filling starts to melt.

6. Plate the enchiladas, drizzle crema all across the top of the enchiladas, and sprinkle with the remaining queso fresco.

CHICKEN ENCHILADAS SUIZAS

Enchiladas Suizas were definitely never on any of my mom's or family's rotation of dinner dishes, but they sure made their way into my belly. These were on the complete opposite side of "authentic Mexican enchiladas." These were more what chain Mexican restaurants offered or what non-Mexican moms brought to the parent-teacher-conference potlucks. Regardless, they were delicious and they've made their way into my rotation of birria dishes.

SERVES 4 to 6

2 cups (480 ml) Tomato Adobo (page 34)

12 corn tortillas

Canola oil

2 cups (480 g) Chicken Birria (page 20)

1 cup (120 g) shredded Chihuahua cheese

1 cup (120 g) shredded Manchego cheese

2 large tomatoes, diced

Finely shredded lettuce

1. Preheat the oven to 375°F (190°C).

2. Heat up the tomato adobo in a small saucepot over medium heat until boiling, about 10 minutes.

3. Line a plate with paper towels. Brush the tortillas with oil and fry in a large frying pan for 35 to 45 seconds per side. Stack on the prepared plate.

4. Add 1 cup (240 ml) of the tomato adobo to the bottom of a 9 x 13-inch (23 x 33 cm) baking dish, making sure to spread it out evenly.

5. Fill the tortillas with chicken birria and roll. Set them in the baking dish and cover with the sauce and remaining adobo. Evenly spread the cheese to the top of the enchiladas.

6. Bake for 25 to 30 minutes or until the cheese has evenly melted. Top with tomatoes and shredded lettuce. Serve right away.

GRILLED CHILES RELLENOS

When I first really started getting into cooking, I became obsessed with grilling. I wanted to master the art of grilling by making every possible dish I could over live fire. This recipe has been in my rotation for more than 15 years, and I still enjoy making it for family and friends alike.

MAKES 6 peppers

One 8-ounce (227 g) package dried corn husks

Oil

6 poblano peppers

1½ cups (360 g) Birria Mother Recipe No. 1 (page 15)

12 ounces (340 g) shredded Chihuahua cheese

1 medium white onion, diced

Salt, to taste

Pepper, to taste

Cilantro, for garnish

1. Fill a large saucepan three-quarters of the way full with water, turn the heat to high, and bring to a boil.

2. Remove the pan from the heat and add the corn husks, making sure to weigh them down with a heatproof bowl and keep submerged for at least 1 hour to rehydrate.

3. Preheat one side of the grill to medium-high. Oil both sides of the grill.

4. Place the poblanos directly over the heat source and cook until blackened but not burnt, about 10 minutes. Flip and cook until the opposite side is also blackened but not burnt, 4 to 6 minutes. Transfer to a large bowl and cover. Allow the poblanos to rest for at least 30 minutes, but up to 2 hours, then run under cold water to remove the blistered skin.

5. Make a slit on each chile and make sure to deseed and devein each poblano. Dry with paper towels and set aside.

6. In another large bowl, mix together the birria, cheese, and onion. Salt and pepper to taste.

7. Use your hands to divide the mixture into 6 portions. Stuff 1 portion into each poblano.

(continued)

8. Choose 12 large corn husks, free of any holes. Lay 6 down and dry with a towel.

9. Lay the stuffed poblanos lengthwise in the middle of the husks and wrap up.

10. Lay out the remaining 6 husks, place the chiles in the husks, tapered end pointing the opposite direction.

11. Tear six ¼-inch (6 mm) strips from the remaining corn husks. Use these strips as ties, fastening them around the center of each corn husk.

12. Cook over indirect heat until slightly charred, about 10 minutes. The cheese should be melted and the birria should be warm.

13. Transfer to a serving plate and cut off the ties. Remove the husks and serve.

CLASSIC CHILES RELLENOS

My Tia Mema makes some of the most delicious and authentic Mexican food I've ever had. Chiles rellenos was a dish I remember having at her house as a kid and absolutely loving. The melty cheese, the crunch of the poblano, and the soft breading make this dish close to perfection for me.

MAKES 6 peppers

6 medium poblano chiles

2 cups (240 g) shredded Chihuahua or Monterey Jack cheese

2 cups (480 g) Birria Mother Recipe No. 1 (page 15)

2 tablespoons (30 ml) vegetable or olive oil, plus more for frying

1 medium onion, chopped into ¼-inch (6 mm) pieces

Three 15-ounce (420 g) cans fire-roasted tomatoes, undrained

2½ cups (600 ml) Birria Consommé (page 28)

2½ teaspoons salt, divided

6 large eggs, separated

2 tablespoons (16 g) all-purpose flour, plus about 1 cup (120 g) for dredging

1. Over a grill, broiler, or any open flame, blister the chiles. Once evenly blistered all over, place in an airtight container and let sit for at least 30 minutes. Under cool water, peel and clean the chiles. Rub off all the blistered skin.

2. Cut a slit in one side (start about ½ inch [1.3 cm] from the top and end about ½ inch [1.3 cm] from the tip). Using your finger, gently dislodge the seeds from the seed pod just below the stem, being careful not to rip the slit all the way to the point. Quickly rinse out the seeds. Drain slit side down on paper towels.

3. In a large bowl mix together the shredded cheese and birria and evenly divide into 6 even portions, using your hands to press each into a compact cylindrical shape.

4. Slide each cylinder of cheese through the slits to fill the chiles, overlap the two sides of the slits, and "sew" them together with a toothpick.

5. Flatten the chiles slightly, lay them on a parchment paper–lined baking sheet and freeze for 1 hour.

6. In a medium saucepan, heat the oil over medium heat, then add the onion and cook for 10 minutes, stirring regularly, until richly golden.

7. Meanwhile, blend the undrained tomatoes on high in a blender until smooth.

8. When the onions are ready, increase the heat to medium-high and add the pureed tomatoes. Cook, stirring often, until it is the consistency of a thick tomato sauce, about 10 minutes.

9. Stir in the consommé, then season with 2 teaspoons of salt. Cover and set aside.

10. In a large skillet over medium-high heat, add the oil and heat to 350ºF (180ºC).

11. Using a mixer, beat the egg whites and the remaining ½ teaspoon salt until stiff peaks form, about 5 minutes. Fold in the yolks, then 2 tablespoons (16 g) of flour.

12. Spread 1 cup (120 g) of flour onto a plate, roll a chile in the flour, shake off the excess, pick it up by the stem, and dip it in the egg white mixture. Make sure it is completely covered.

13. In one swift move, pull the chile out of the batter and gently lay it in the hot oil. Work in batches, placing the chiles in a single layer in the frying pan. Gently baste the peppers with hot oil from the skillet as they cook. Cook until deep golden, about 4 minutes. Turn and cook for 4 more minutes or until both sides are deep golden in color, then transfer to a plate lined with paper towels.

Tortillas and Their Cousins

CORN TORTILLAS

Homemade corn tortillas are some of the most delicious and satisfying things to add to your culinary arsenal. When I would visit my family in Mexico, it seemed we always had tortillas with almost every meal simply because of the fact that every neighborhood seemed to have a tortilleria, so you would get warm, fresh tortillas every time. When I learned how easy it was to make tortillas at home, it was game over. No more store-bought tortillas with their never-ending list of ingredients and science lab words I can't pronounce.

MAKES 12 tortillas

1 cup (240 ml) warm water

1½ cups (190 g) masa harina

2 teaspoons kosher salt

1. Slowly add the warm water to the dry masa flour in a bowl while constantly stirring. Add the salt and stir.

2. Knead until the water is evenly incorporated and no dry, powdery spots remain. Tortilla masa should be moist to the touch but not tacky. If the dough becomes too wet, add a bit more masa.

3. Heat a comal or large skillet over medium-high heat.

4. Roll the masa into 12 ping-pong–size balls.

5. Using a tortilla press, flatten the ball in between two sheets of wax paper.

6. Lay the tortilla on the hot comal or skillet and cook for 20 to 30 seconds. Flip and repeat. Flip one more time and cook until the tortilla begins to puff up, 5 to 10 seconds. Transfer to a kitchen towel and keep warm, repeating the process with the remaining dough.

FLOUR TORTILLAS

I have been judged my entire life for loving flour tortillas as much as I do. My friend, Chef Claudia Sandoval, even accused me of being a fake Mexican (it was all in good fun—she just couldn't believe I pick flour over corn tortillas). There is no shame in my flour tortilla game!

MAKES 6 tortillas

3 cups (375 g) all-purpose flour

1 teaspoon salt

2 teaspoons baking powder

⅓ cup (80 g) lard

1 cup (240 ml) hot water

1. In a large bowl, combine the flour, salt, and baking powder. Stir with your fingers.

2. Add the lard and stir until pea-size crumbles form.

3. Slowly add the water and start stirring the dough with your hands in the bowl (it will be very sticky at first). When the dough starts coming together, transfer to a clean, flat work surface.

4. Knead the dough for 10 minutes or until the dough is smooth.

5. Divide into 6 balls of dough, cover with a moist paper towel, and let rest for up to 30 minutes.

6. Grab a rolling pin and start forming the tortillas on a lightly floured surface. Press slightly with your hand, set the rolling pin at the center of the ball, and press forward without making it to the edge and then press back toward yourself, stopping before the edge. Turn the tortilla 45 degrees and repeat pressing forward and then toward you. Flip the tortilla and repeat the same process until you have a thin disk about 12 inches (30 cm) in diameter.

GORDITAS

Directly translated, *gordita* means "chubby" in Mexico. Gorditas are exactly that: chubby little tortillas that make fun vessels for a birria snack. Unlike a tortilla, gorditas are cut open on one side in order to be filled with ingredients.

MAKES 6 gorditas

DOUGH

1 cup (125 g) masa harina

1 cup (240 ml) warm water

1 teaspoon salt

FILLING

1 cup (240 g) Birria Mother Recipe No. 1 (page 15)

1 tomato, seeded and diced

1 cup (30 g) finely shredded lettuce

2 tablespoons (30 g) sour cream

2 tablespoons (15 g) cotija cheese

MAKE THE DOUGH

1. Slowly add the warm water to the dry masa flour in a bowl while constantly stirring. Stir in the salt.

2. Knead until the water is evenly incorporated and no dry, powdery spots remain. The masa should be moist to the touch but not tacky. If it's too wet, add a bit more masa.

3. Heat a comal or large skillet over medium-high heat.

4. Roll the masa into 6 ping-pong–size balls.

5. Using a tortilla press, flatten the ball in between two sheets of wax paper, making sure not to press it down too much as it will become too thin. You want it to be about twice as thick as a normal tortilla.

6. Lay the tortilla on the hot comal or skillet and sear for 10 to 15 seconds. Flip and cook for 10 to 15 seconds more. Flip one more time and cook until brown spots appear, about 1 minute. The gordita will begin to inflate and bubble up in the center or sides. Lightly press down on the sides of the gordita with a spatula to help it inflate even more. Remove it from the griddle, place it on a plate, and cover it with a kitchen towel. Repeat with the remaining dough.

FILL THE GORDITAS

1. As soon as the gordita has cooled down enough to be handled, use a knife to cut a slit down the edge of one side of the gordita. Fill with an even amount of your ingredients.

SOPES

When made correctly, a good sope will be equally as soft as it is crispy, making it an excellent vessel for your birria. Also, keep it simple by not overdoing it with the toppings. For this recipe, let the birria set the stage for the sope to be the star of the show.

SERVES 8 sopes

1¾ cups (220 g) masa harina

1 cup (240 ml) plus 2 tablespoons (30 ml) warm water

½ teaspoon salt

2 tablespoons (28 g) lard or vegetable oil

1 teaspoon baking powder

¼ cup (30 g) flour

Vegetable oil, for frying

1 cup (240 g) Birria Mother Recipe No. 1 (page 15)

½ cup (120 g) Pressure Cooker Refried Beans (page 146)

¼ cup (60 g) Mexican crema

¼ cup (35 g) Mexipoix (page 147)

¼ cup (30 g) shredded cotija cheese

¼ cup (60 ml) Habanero Salsa (page 42)

1. Heat a comal or griddle over medium heat.

2. In a large bowl, slowly add the warm water to the dry masa flour while stirring. Add in the salt and stir.

3. Knead until the water is evenly incorporated and soft and moist to the touch. It will be tacky but not sticky.

4. Mix in the lard or oil, baking powder, and flour.

5. Divide into 4 portions, roll into balls, and flatten into fat disks that are 3 inches (7.5 cm) wide and a little over 1 inch (2.5 cm) thick.

6. Lay on the hot comal or griddle and cook for 4 minutes or until browned. Flip and repeat. At this point, the masa will not be cooked through. Transfer the sopes to a plate to cool for 10 minutes.

7. Once cooled, evenly split the soft masa disk in half, cooked side down.

8. Using your fingers, create a ¾-inch (2 cm)-tall wall or lip around the edge of the sope. Make sure the wall is even all the way around and the bottom is flat in order for it to cook evenly.

9. Fill a large saucepan with about 1 inch (2.5 cm) of vegetable oil and heat to 350°F (180°C) over medium-high heat.

10. Place as many sopes as you can into a skillet. Cook until golden, 2 to 3 minutes. Remove from the oil and place upside down on a paper towel–lined plate. Let cool.

11. Transfer to a plate and layer each with birria, refried beans, a drizzle of Mexican crema and Mexipoix, then sprinkle some cotija cheese over the top for the perfect Insta pic. Serve with habanero salsa.

TOSTADAS

Tostadas taught me what texture could add to a dish. I will never forget eating tostadas at a food stand on the side of the road that my dad had taken me to. My nine-year-old mind was blown at how much there was going on. There was warm shredded chicken topped with cool crema, wet lettuce, and tomatoes all atop the crunchiest tostada. With this recipe I tried to recreate that memory and did my best to play a time-traveling warlock that goes back in time to make a perfect food memory even more perfect.

MAKES 10 tostadas

Vegetable oil

10 Corn Tortillas (page 134)

2½ cups (600 g) Pressure Cooker Refried Beans (page 146)

2 cups (480 g) Chicken Birria (page 20)

4 cups (120 g) shredded lettuce

2 cups (360 g) finely diced tomato

2 cups (240 g) shredded Chihuahua or Monterey Jack cheese

5 tablespoons (75 ml) Habanero Salsa (page 42)

5 tablespoons (75 ml) Mexican crema

5 tablespoons (75 g) Classic Guacamole (page 36)

½ cup (8 g) chopped fresh cilantro

10 lime wedges

1. Heat ½ cup (120 ml) of vegetable oil in a large frying pan over medium heat until it reads 350°F (180°C) on an instant-read thermometer.

2. Fry each tortilla for about 2 minutes, frequently flipping and replacing oil as needed. Once crisp and golden, transfer to a plate lined with paper towels. Let cool 2 to 3 minutes.

3. To assemble tostadas, evenly spread about ⅓ cup (80 g) of the refried beans on each tostada shell and top with chicken birria, lettuce, tomato, and shredded cheese.

4. Drizzle with salsa and crema, then add a dollop of guacamole to each. Garnish with cilantro and serve with lime wedges.

CHAPTER 8

Sides

MAMA'S ARROZ

My mom's rice is one of my absolute favorite things in the world to eat. She would always say that the secret ingredient was love, and now that I don't live close to her, I realize that it was true. I love my mama and I love this rice. Make sure to use the secret ingredient.

SERVES 4

1 cup (195 g) jasmine rice

Olive oil

½ onion, diced

4 cloves garlic, minced

1 cup (240 ml) tomato sauce

2 cups (480 ml) chicken broth

1 chicken bouillon cube (Knorr bouillon is the secret weapon in most Mexican kitchens)

1. In a medium stockpot over medium heat, fry the rice in olive oil for about 8 minutes or until lightly golden. Add the onion and garlic and cook, stirring, until fragrant, about 5 minutes.

2. Add the tomato sauce and stir. Add the chicken broth and bouillon cube.

3. Bring to a simmer, stir, and lower heat to low. Cover and simmer 10 minutes or until liquid is mostly absorbed.

PICKLED RED ONIONS

Pickled red onions are a culinary cheat code. You want to make the most bland food creation look appealing? Throw some pickled red onions on there. But not only do they add good looks, they have the perfect amount of tang and brine to level up whatever you put them on.

SERVES 6

2 red onions, finely sliced

Ice water

1 tablespoon (5 g) dried Mexican oregano

1 teaspoon coarse kosher salt

2 tablespoons (30 ml) white wine vinegar

Juice of ½ lime

1. Fill a medium saucepan with water and bring to a boil over high heat.

2. Add the onion and cook for 1 minute. Drain and drop onion into ice water to stop the cooking process.

3. Drain the onions, place into a glass bowl, and add the oregano, salt, vinegar, and lime juice. Stir.

CURTIDO

These pickled habanero peppers and red onion have a tart and tangy flavor thanks to the two kinds of vinegar and lime juice. This condiment is great served alongside birria or atop tacos and burritos. Play around with the flavors and add spices to your liking. This recipe is a canvas for anything you want to try.

MAKES 3 cups (720 ml)

4 habanero peppers, thinly sliced

1 large red onion, thinly sliced

2 cloves garlic, minced

½ cup (120 ml) apple cider vinegar

½ cup (120 ml) white vinegar

½ cup (120 ml) freshly squeezed lime juice

½ cup (120 ml) water

1 tablespoon (15 g) pure maple syrup or granulated sugar

1 teaspoon kosher salt

1. In a large bowl, toss together the habaneros, red onion, and garlic. Transfer the habanero mixture to a large quart jar with a lid, pushing it down into the jar. Leave ¼ inch (6 mm) of headspace at the top of the jar.

2. In a small saucepan, combine the remaining ingredients and heat until boiling. Remove from the burner and pour over the onions and peppers until covering them completely. Place the lid on the jar and let them sit until cool and then refrigerate until ready to use.

3. You can serve these the day they are made, but they are best made the day before.

PRESSURE COOKER REFRIED BEANS

I wish I had a time machine so I could go back to when my little abuela was spending too much time making refried beans and hand her an Instant Pot (or other brand of electric pressure cooker), giving her back countless hours that she could have used to spend looking off into the sea, which she loved to do.

SERVES 4

2 pounds (907 g) dried pinto beans

1 large onion, diced

5 cloves garlic

12 cups (2.8 L) chicken broth

One 8-ounce (227 g) can diced green chiles

4 bay leaves

4 teaspoons (12 g) ground cumin

½ chicken bouillon cube

7 tablespoons (105 g) lard

1. Combine all the ingredients except the lard in an electric pressure cooker and set to high pressure for 35 minutes, making sure the valve is set to sealed.

2. Once cooked, allow natural release on the pressure cooker for 15 minutes, then open the valve for manual release.

3. Discard the bay leaves and strain 4 to 5 cups (960 to 1200 ml) of liquid from the beans and reserve.

4. In a food processor, blend the beans to a smooth consistency, adding reserve liquid as needed.

5. Melt the lard in a large pot over medium heat.

6. Add the beans to the pot and cook over low heat, allowing the flavors to develop and the beans to thicken slightly more.

MEXIPOIX (MEXICAN MIREPOIX)

On a very hangover-y Sunday morning during football season, I arrived at my friend Kevin Leary's house with a bag full of quesabirria supplies, so I thought. His wife and my good friend, Stephanie, noticed that my bag had only birria, cheese, and tortillas. I panicked. I had somehow forgotten the rest of the ingredients I was going to top my quesabirria with.

Kevin told me to worry about making the quesabirria, assuring me that he would handle it. What Kevin created that day is a topping that I call Mexipoix—and I now refuse to make and eat quesabirria without it. It's a beautiful symphony of briny, citrusy, and bright flavors that expertly cut through the overly rich bites of quesabirria. Kevin's topping makes its way into so many recipes not only in this book but in my everyday cooking.

SERVES 10

1 large red onion, finely diced

1 bunch cilantro, finely chopped

One 12-ounce (340 g) can pickled jalapeño slices, drained

Juice of 1 lime

1. In a medium bowl, toss together the onion, cilantro, jalapeño, and lime juice. Store in an airtight container in the refrigerator for up to a week.

QUESO FUNDIDO

I will never forget the first time I ever tasted queso fundido. It was the late 80s and I was a kid watching *Miami Vice* with my parents. My mom wanted to make a quick snack, so she whipped up some queso fundido. It was so simple, just really cheesy and rich in the most delicious way. She made hers with chorizo and I'm my own person, so this version is made with my beef birria and a few more ingredients than hers. Still though, thanks, Mom, for the inspo.

SERVES 4

2 tablespoons (30 ml) vegetable oil

1 large white onion, finely chopped

½ cup (120 g) Birria Mother Recipe No. 1 (page 15)

¼ cup (60 ml) cold water

1 tablespoon (8 g) all-purpose flour

2 cups (480 ml) Birria Starter (page 29)

1 teaspoon salt

1 pound (454 g) freshly grated Chihuahua cheese

Chopped fresh cilantro, for garnish

Finely diced tomato, for garnish

Toasted pepitas, for garnish

Totopos (page 151)

1. Preheat the oven to 425°F (220°C).

2. Heat 1 tablespoon (15 ml) of the oil in a Dutch oven over medium-high heat. Add the onions and cook, stirring occasionally, until the onions begin to caramelize, about 10 minutes. Set aside.

3. Place the birria and cooked onions in a 12-inch (30 cm) cast-iron skillet.

4. Whisk together the cold water and flour in a small saucepan. Add ½ cup (120 ml) of the birria starter and salt. Stir. Simmer over medium-low heat until the mixture is thickened, about 3 minutes. Add the mixture to the beef and onions in the skillet. Sprinkle with the cheese. Bake until bubbly, about 15 minutes.

5. Sprinkle with the cilantro, tomatoes, and pepitas before serving with totopos.

NASHVILLE QUESO

Queso is Spanish for cheese. Simple. Don't try telling Texans and Nashvillians that, though. Queso to them is liquid gold, a cheese-ish dip that they pour over chips and anything else they possibly can. When I first moved to Nashville, I hated queso. Everything about it made me grumpy. But as time went on, I softened and realized what it meant to some folks. It was a beloved snack and topping. Heck, there is a self-proclaimed Queso Queen in town (Hi, Delia Jo)!

I skipped the grumpiness and went with the flow. Now I find myself asking for queso at restaurants and making it to complement some of my more fun food creations. You can garnish it with cilantro, tomatoes, or whatever your heart desires.

MAKES about 4 cups (960 ml)

1½ cups (360 ml) evaporated milk

1 tablespoon (8 g) cornstarch

12 ounces (340 g) white American cheese, finely chopped

4 ounces (113 g) mozzarella cheese, freshly shredded

2 tablespoons (18 g) chopped canned jalapeños

1 teaspoon chili powder

1 teaspoon red pepper flakes

¼ teaspoon salt

¼ teaspoon black pepper

1. Heat evaporated milk over medium-high heat in a small saucepan. Stir in the cornstarch and whisk to combine. Bring to a simmer and immediately reduce heat to low.

2. Stir in the cheese in batches, starting with the white American cheese. As you stir in the cheese, increase the heat to medium-low and whisk, stirring constantly while the cheese melts. Once all the cheese is melted, stir in the jalapeños, chili powder, red pepper, and salt and pepper.

TOTOPOS (HOMEMADE TORTILLA CHIPS)

Homemade corn tortilla chips are so incredibly easy to make that you'll never want to use store-bought ever again. It's also a great way to use stale tortillas. Make sure to use corn tortillas that are not made with a ton of unnecessary ingredients. Tortillas made with anything more than corn, water, and lime (calcium hydroxide) will not fry well and might turn out soggy instead of crispy.

SERVES 4

½ cup (120 ml) vegetable oil

12 corn tortillas (see Note)

Salt, to taste

Paprika (optional)

1. Using a sharp knife, cut the tortillas into small triangles.

2. In a large frying pan, bring oil to 350°F (180°C) over medium-high heat. You can test with a chip. If the oil sizzles when you put the chip in, you're good to go.

3. Work in batches, adding the tortilla triangles to the pan in a single layer.

4. Fry until golden and crispy, 1 to 2 minutes on each side. Add more oil if necessary.

5. Transfer the chips to a paper towel–lined plate and season immediately with salt and paprika while still hot.

NOTE: Old, stale tortillas work best.

BLOODY MARIA AND MICHELADA MIX

One of my favorite cocktail bars in Nashville is a very great and unassuming spot called Otto's Bar. Their staff whips up some gems without the pomp and circumstance of any overly curated, "hot right now" space. They're consistently good and the staff is top-notch.

I worked with Otto's for a brunch event and their manager, Bode Craig, had come up with a very impressive lineup of cocktails for the event. I mentioned to him an idea I had for a birria michelada and Bode was off and running. I personally felt I already had a great michelada mix recipe, but Bode's slapped mine back to the minor leagues.

SERVES 8

MIX

2 cups (280 g) diced vine-ripened tomato

3 cups (720 ml) organic tomato juice

2 cups (480 ml) Birria Starter (page 29)

1 tablespoon (18 g) salt

½ white onion, chopped

2 tablespoons (12 g) black pepper

1 tablespoon (5 g) cayenne powder

¼ cup (16 g) minced fresh dill

⅓ cup (80 ml) Worcestershire sauce

2 tablespoons (30 g) vinegar-based hot sauce

½ cup (85 g) crushed fresh pineapple

2 tablespoons (30 g) prepared horseradish

¼ cup (38 g) diced green bell pepper

¼ cup (60 ml) fresh lime juice

GARNISHES

Brunch style: celery, olives of choice, and thinly sliced cured meat

For strained drinks and stemware: lemon slice and marinated olives

Fancy: sprinkle of smoked sea salt and drizzle of extra-virgin olive oil

MAKE THE MIX

1. Place all ingredients in a blender and pulse until the desired consistency is reached. Strain with a fine-mesh strainer, if desired.

MAKE A BLOODY MARIA OR MICHELADA

1. To make a Bloody Maria, add 2 ounces (60 ml) Reposado and 4 ounces (120 ml) of the mix, stir, and serve over ice. To make a michelada, add 1 ounce (30 ml) of the mix, ½ ounce (15 ml) Mezcal, then top with pilsner or Mexican Lager. Serve with a salt and Tajín rim.

Acknowledgments

Where do I start?

To my soulmate, Audrey. Without you, I'm incomplete and with you, I can do anything I set my mind to. Thank you for your being the best, most patient, and my all-time ride-or-die. (I finally have an emergency contact that isn't my mom.)

To my mama, Alicia. I don't know where I'd be without your unconditional love. You're truly an angel and everything I do will always be dedicated to you.

To my siblings Erika, Adrian, and Daniela. You are the best support system a big brother could ask for. I will always strive to make you proud to be my siblings.

To the Rezendez clan: Thin Bones, Lady Di, Max and Alec. Y'all are the best, but you still owe me a visit in Nashville. Knock knock, it's Jesus!

To Rick, Melissa, and Victor Linus: Rick, there's not a day that goes by that I don't miss you. I know this book would have gotten a "fuck yeah!" out of you.

To Jacob Sembrano, my other brother: Thank you for always giving me the brilliantly thoughtful and honest feedback that pushes me to be a better cook. But, most importantly, for teaching me to embrace "jazz cooking."

To John Carruthers and John Scholl: One my life's greatest joys has been cooking, creating, and constantly joking with you. I love you dudes. Tré J 4-ever.

To Mark, Kate, and Peter Danger Slonina: I'm a lucky dude to have you as my extended family.

To all of the amazing people that shared their recipes for this book: I'm eternally grateful for your contributions. Thank you for making me look good. ;)

I'm sure I'm going to forget too many people, so make sure to call me out when you read this if I do: The Valenciana, Sutherland, Scholl, Carruthers, Romero, Reens, Walling, O'Shea, and Whitecorn families. Cousin Ricky and fam, Aubrey Boonstra, Sarah and Sean, Julio Hernandez and the Maiz de la Vida fam, Claudia Sandoval, Aaron and Christen, Brandon Frohne, Davis Reese, Arjuna Patel, the Awad Brothers, Ryan and Ashley, Anne and Paul, Tori "Tor Hammer," Marisa and Tony, Burger Kerns, Tina Spurr, JP Murphy, Mikey and Chris, Mikey and Ashley, Richie Klatzco, Ben and Xtina, Splinter, Bob, Kyle and Flip, Betsy Cashen, Clint and Emily, the Barrique Crew, Tyler Martin, Alex Vogt, Jonathan Moxey, Dan Heaghney, Phil Wymore. I love you all.

To my publisher, The Quarto Group, specifically Dan Rosenberg: Thank you for taking a chance on me. To the best photographer, Clayton Hauck: I'm lucky to have such a talent like yourself be a part of this.

Writing a book is not easy, but it's a fun-ass ride. From people I just met to those I've known my entire life: In one way or another, you continue to inspire me to make better food, so I thank you.

About the Author

JESSE VALENCIANA, a reporter and columnist for *The Takeout,* is one of the premier food journalists focused on Mexican cuisine and other Hispanic foods of the Americas. He also presides over Nashville's hippest catering and pop-up company, The Secret Bodega. A veteran of several prestigious restaurant kitchens and a former marketing executive with Goose Island Brewery, he has appeared on *The Today Show* and on local television segments in Chicago and Nashville, among other cities. His experience with birrias spans from eating his grandmother's traditional birria every Sunday as a child to collaborating with leading chefs on novel birria creations today.

Index